ILLUSTRATED

HOUSEBUILDING

with respect to all the old Carpenters
who originally figured it out

Graham Blackburn

ILLUSTRATED HOUSEBUILDING

The House that .... Built

BONANZA BOOKS · NEW YORK

BONANZA 1978 PRINTING

PREFACE.

More than a century has elapsed since an ingenious and useful work on the Arts connected with Building was published under the title of MECHANICAL EXERCISES by the celebrated JOSEPH MOXON: that it was both useful and popular the various editions testify, and at this time it is become scarce and rarely to be met with. It can be no disparagement to its ingenious author, to say, that the progress of science, and the changes in matters of art have rendered the work obsolete...

Peter Nicholson, 1812

from the Preface to Peter Nicholson's book,

Mechanical Exercises; or, the
Elements And Practice of
Carpentry, Joinery, Bricklaying, etc..

ACKNOWLEDGEMENTS

Even a work of fiction is the result of an author's experience, and as such owes a large debt for its creation to all the other people who have played a part in the author's life. A book of facts is even more the result of other people, for it is an objective account of their discoveries and actions in their lives and on their surroundings rather than a subjective account of their influence upon the author's personal story. Therefore, it would be most ungrateful and unrealistic were I not to mention the people in my life who have helped to make this book possible.

I would like to thank my father, who taught me the right attitude; Harris, who taught me respect for the craft; R.J. Puttick, who taught me that form was as important as function, and that we would all build houses one day; Lubinsky, who brought me to the right place; Holly & Teddy, who provided me with the opportunity; Heide and Oliver, who demonstrated the necessity and rewards of necessities; Elaine, who proved them; and lastly, all the craftsmen of Woodstock who offered criticism, advice, and encouragement.

CONTENTS

A LIST OF THE FRAMED ILLUSTRATIONS

INTRODUCTION

Gone are the days when trades were learned with seven year apprenticeships, which like everything else, is partly good and partly bad. In this case good because it gives us more leisure, but bad because while techniques and materials may have become more sophisticated the level of enduring craftsmanship has dropped. So while I have tried to explain the standards and techniques for building a substantial, well-built house, it should be realized that these are no longer the only criteria. Many houses are built primarily for immediate profit, and so economy and speed are often more important considerations than durability or beauty.

Illustrated Housebuilding presents essentially the method used in building the standard frame house, a direct descendant of early colonial and pioneer houses, which were developed from European models adapted to a new environment and different requirements. However, any step, once understood in itself and in relation to the other steps involved, may be modified in an almost limitless number of ways.

AMERICAN COLONIAL HOUSE

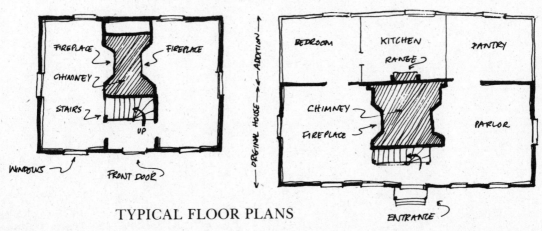

TYPICAL FLOOR PLANS

The order of steps may be changed to a certain extent. The dimensions, while basically a function of such things as standard lumber sizes and building codes, may be changed to suit your own taste and convenience. The point is that while the method may be basically similar, the designs may vary considerably. It is only necessary to look around at other buildings to see that while the majority are all constructed on the same principles as explained in this book, hardly any two look exactly alike.

It is important to remember that while each chapter is complete in itself, to be completely understood it should be read in context with the rest of the book. Read the whole book first before attempting any one stage and you will have a better idea of what you are doing, and why.

The final point I would like to make is that this is a basic method, and not a definitive encyclopedia of all possible ways of housebuilding. Therefore, at the end of each chapter there is a relevant bibliography containing sources for more specialized information for each stage of construction.

CHAPTER ONE. *Site and Foundation*

THE SITE

The very first thing to think about once you have decided to build a house is *where* to build it. Here is a list of things to consider:

1. The Axis of the House.
2. The Slope of the Land.
3. Drainage.
4. Water Supply.
5. Access.
6. View.
7. Internal Functions.
8. Privacy & Neighbors.

1. The Axis of the House.

You will want to consider how the house lies—that is, which way is front and back, and which are the sides, and how the whole thing sits in relation to the sun. If you build in the Northern Hemisphere remember that the part of the house facing South gets sun all day long. If you like being awakened by the early morning sun, build the bedrooms on the Eastern side. North light is best for studios. If you live in a snow area, it helps to have the front door on the Southern side—the snow melts quickest here.

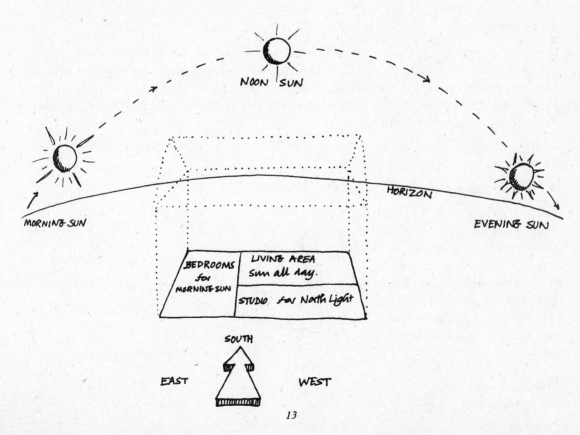

2. The Slope of the Land.

Unless your land is perfectly flat the slope will affect things. If it is very steep there will be more foundation work and you will have to think carefully about floor levels and entrances—but you will also have greater opportunity for balconies.

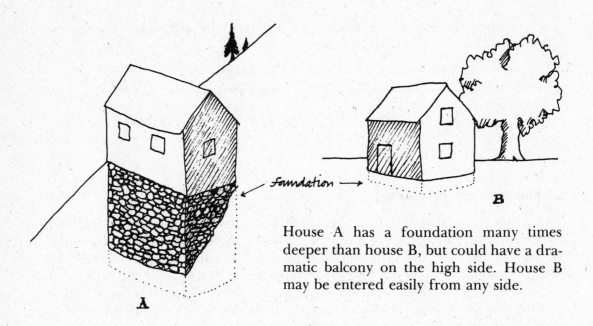

House A has a foundation many times deeper than house B, but could have a dramatic balcony on the high side. House B may be entered easily from any side.

3. Drainage.

Try and choose a dry spot to build on. It will make the foundation work much easier if you do not have to excavate in a marsh! A dry, gently sloping area will be better for your sewage system than a flat, boggy area. Remember also, if you are inspecting the land in the summer, that many dry stream beds become raging torrents during the rest of the year.

4. Water Supply.

Locating the house downhill from an available water supply such as a spring or a stream can save a lot of money on wells, pumps and pressure tanks. But be sure the spring or stream will not dry up if it doesn't rain for a while!

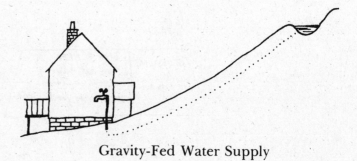

Gravity-Fed Water Supply

5. Access.

Remember that no matter how well the location of the site fulfills all other conditions you must be able to get to it. It is, of course, possible to carry everything in by hand if you decide to build deep in the woods or high on a mountain, but it is much easier if there is easy access to the road. It helps a lot if trucks can deliver material right to the site. If you live in a snow area remember that the cost of having your driveway plowed in the winter increases with its length—the driveway's and the winter's. Remember too that it is hard to drive (and walk, especially with groceries) up a long, steep driveway covered with ice in mid-winter.

Unless you aim to be primitive or maintain your own generator bear in mind that it is expensive to bring in electricity. Utility companies require poles for overhead power lines every 150 feet or so, and it is becoming mandatory in more and more areas to install underground "service" or power lines, which is even more expensive—although it looks better, lasts longer and is not subject to damage by wind, snow or ice. So the nearer you can build to an existing power supply the cheaper it will be.

6. View.

In the past, people who built houses in the country generally spent most of their time out of doors and consequently were not concerned with "bringing the outdoors indoors." They also did not have insulated windows and so the fewer they had, and the smaller they were, the easier it was to keep the house warm. Nowadays, however, this is not the case, and a good view can add much pleasure, as well as value, to a house.

7. Internal Functions.

How you plan to use the house can affect where you locate it and how you design the inside. For instance, workshops are more conveniently situated at ground level where deliveries may be made easily. Bedrooms are better on the quiet side of the house. The view may be nicest from the living area, and so on.

8. Privacy and Neighbors.

If you enjoy privacy don't build near your property boundaries unless you are certain the adjacent land is not going to be developed. Remember too that deciduous trees lose their leaves in winter and you may then discover neighbors who were invisible all summer.

IMPORTANT! Check out the legal requirements explained in the Appendix—these may also affect where you build.

THE FOUNDATION

Many early American buildings were constructed almost without foundations. One or two courses (layers, in masonry) of rough stone, picked from the fields, were simply laid on top of the ground, and this formed the base for the whole building. No excavation was attempted and the only reason for the stones was to prevent the bottom of the walls from rotting on the wet ground. Over the years, however, the ground settles and the frost and ice work on the stones until the sills (the bottom beams of the house) do come in contact with the ground where they rot out and cause the building to fall over or collapse. There are a few of these buildings, mostly barns, still standing, but for all practical purposes there are really only two ways of starting a house. One is to build a house on **PIERS**, and the other is to build a house on a **FULL FOUNDATION**.

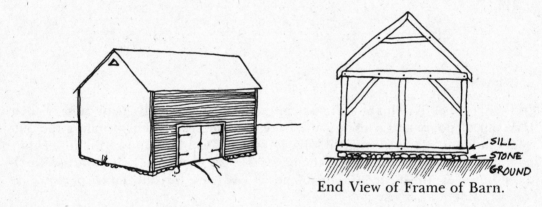

A Barn built right on the Ground.

End View of Frame of Barn.

PIERS are simply legs stuck in the ground on which the house stands!

A House built on Piers.

Piers may be made of laid up stone, concrete block, reinforced concrete, metal or just plain timber posts. Locust posts * are the best if wood is used; they are extremely resistant to rot. Piers are good for building in marshy ground, sandy ground or water.

The Florida Indians who live in the Everglades build their houses on piers.

* Posts made from the wood of the Locust tree.

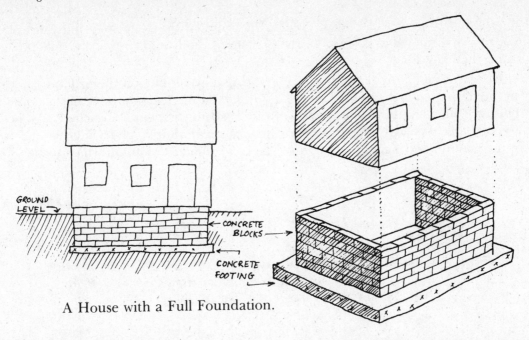

A House with a Full Foundation.

FULL FOUNDATIONS are best; they are not likely to tilt or fall over as piers sometimes do; they provide better insulation for the underside of the house; they provide a protected space for the "works" of a house, i.e., the furnace, the electrical wiring and most of the plumbing; they may be used as garages, extra rooms or simply for storage space; and one last advantage, banks are often more willing to make loans on houses with full foundations.

CONSTRUCTION OF A FULL FOUNDATION

The construction of the foundation may be dealt with in four stages:

1. Locating the Building Lines.
2. Excavating.
3. Making the Footings.
4. Building the Foundation Walls.

1. Locating the Building Lines.

Having chosen the site for the house the exact location of the foundation must now be determined. However, if the ground is not clear you will save much time and expense by cutting down anything which is growing and stacking the resultant brush somewhere neatly away from the site. If there is anything bigger than 3″ (inches) in diameter leave about 18″ of it standing—it makes it easier for the bulldozer to push out.

There are two lines which must now be determined: the excavation line, and the line marking the exact position of the outside of the foundation walls, sometimes called the "face line".

The excavation line may be shown by pouring garden lime on the ground where the bulldozer is to dig. This line should be about 3' (feet) outside the face line. The face line should be indicated with line (string or twine) stretched taut between "batter boards". A batter board may be made simply by driving two stakes in the ground and nailing a horizontal piece of wood to them on which to tie the line.

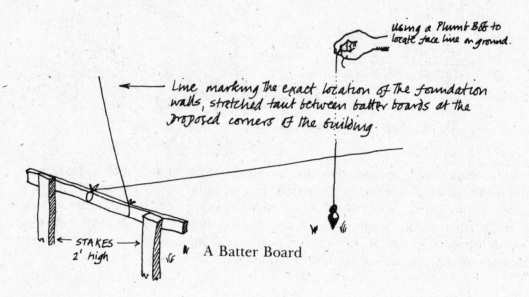

using a Plumb Bob to locate face line on ground.

Line marking the exact location of the foundation walls, stretched taut between batter boards at the proposed corners of the building.

STAKES 2' high

A Batter Board

Too much care cannot be taken in ensuring that the face line is exactly located. A simple way of checking, for small rectangular buildings, is first to make sure that the opposite sides are equal and then to measure the diagonals. If the diagonals are equal then the corners will be perfect right angles (i.e. 90°), and the building will be "square."

2. Excavating.

You must now hire a man with a bulldozer to excavate the area you have indicated with the lime. Digging it out yourself with pickax, shovel and wheelbarrow is possible, but would take you weeks: (One reason why the old guys sometimes built straight on the ground!)

The bulldozer should excavate the area so that the bottom is as flat and level as possible and at least one foot below the **FROST LINE.**

The **FROST LINE** is the depth to which frost reaches. Below this line the ground, rarely freezing, stays firm and the house will rest securely on this ground. If the

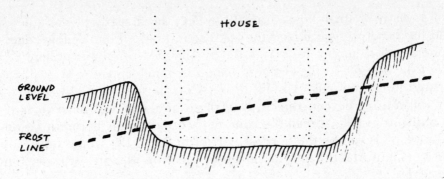

house foundations are built above this line, the ground below may freeze and in so doing move and heave, breaking the foundation and making the house unsafe! The NATIONAL BUILDING CODE requires a minimum of 1'-0" (one foot) below Frost Line. Local Building Codes will tell you how deep the frost line is in your area. Should you encounter bedrock—solid rock—before you reach the appropriate depth you may stop there since bedrock will not move no matter how cold it gets. Even if you build where there is no freezing weather you should still be at least 1'-6" below "grade" (ground level) to assure a firm and level base for the house.

3. Making the Footings.

The FOOTING is a small but wide concrete platform running around the proposed perimeter of the building on which the foundation wall will rest. It is made at least a third wider than the foundation wall in order to distribute the load to be borne over a wider area and so prevent settling.

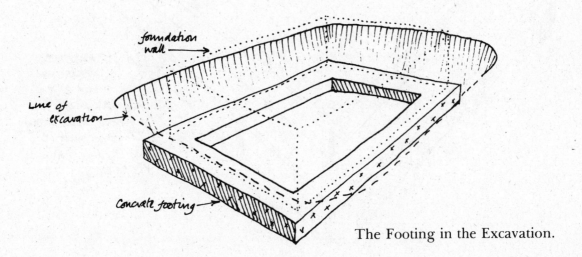

The Footing in the Excavation.

The footing is made with concrete which is best delivered to the site ready mixed in a large truck by a firm which specializes in this. Once again, you could mix it yourself but the footings will be much stronger if poured all at the same time, and even for a relatively small house, say 20' by 30', the first batch would be "set up" (dry and hard) before you mixed the last batch. Look in the Yellow Pages of the telephone directory under "Concrete-Ready Mixed" to find a supplier. Tell them the size of the house and they will estimate how much concrete you will need. (It is calculated in cubic yards.) Unless *all* parts of the footing are accessible by the truck it will dump the concrete in one place and you will have to have some friends on hand to help spread the concrete around evenly before it becomes too stiff to move. This can be the hardest part of building the whole house, and it is also the most important, being in all senses the "foundation" of everything else. So be ready!

The concrete is poured into a form—a temporary wooden "mold," which is removed after the concrete is hard. Concrete must be protected against quick drying if cracks and structural weaknesses (not always visible) are to be avoided. Leaving the forms on for a few days after the concrete has been poured is generally sufficient protection. Actually the concrete continues "curing" or drying and hardening for many years.

The form for the concrete is easily built; a typical form is shown below.

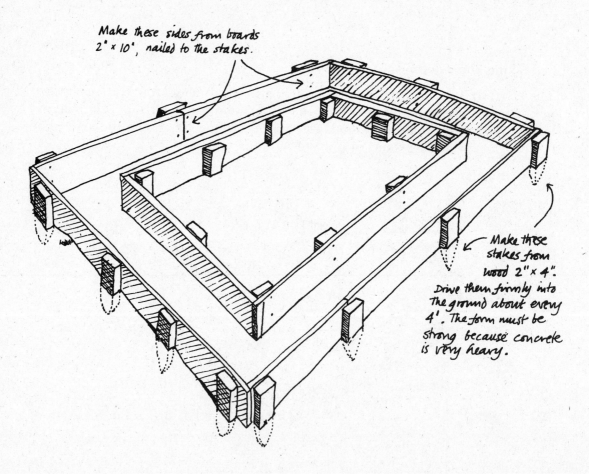

Make these sides from boards 2" x 10", nailed to the stakes.

Make these stakes from wood 2" x 4". Drive them firmly into the ground about every 4'. The form must be strong because concrete is very heavy.

Use the longest boards 2" thick by 10" wide (commonly referred to as 2" x 10" 's) you can find. Lumberyards usually carry them in 12', 14', 16' and sometimes 18' lengths. Stand them on edge and nail them firmly to 2' stakes made from sharpened pieces of 2" x 4" lumber.

Assuming you are going to build the foundation wall with concrete blocks 8" wide, remember that the footing should be at least ⅓ again as wide, so make the two sides of the form about 16" apart to be safe. Use the plumb bob hanging from the face line, as shown before, to position the forms.

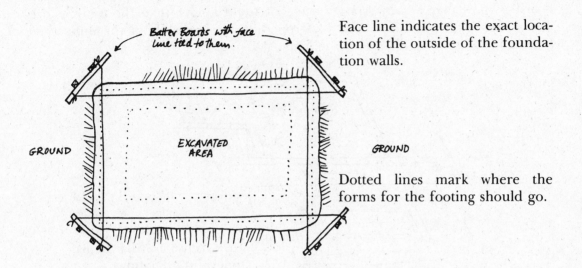

Face line indicates the exact location of the outside of the foundation walls.

Dotted lines mark where the forms for the footing should go.

It is most important to make sure that the forms are PERFECTLY level; otherwise the footings will be sloping and you will have a hard time trying to make the foundation walls level, and in turn, the house itself! The excavator usually has instruments such as transits and Y levels and will have made the bottom of the hole pretty flat, but you must level up the tops of the forms using a long spirit level on the boards. It is also a good idea to stretch a line, tied to the tops of the form, diagonally, from one corner to the other, and hang a line level on it.

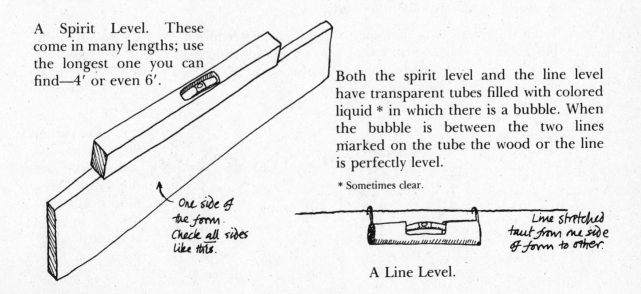

A Spirit Level. These come in many lengths; use the longest one you can find—4' or even 6'.

Both the spirit level and the line level have transparent tubes filled with colored liquid * in which there is a bubble. When the bubble is between the two lines marked on the tube the wood or the line is perfectly level.

* Sometimes clear.

A Line Level.

When the forms have been built and you are satisfied they are stout, properly positioned and level, you will be ready for the concrete. Hope for a dry, warm day and arm yourself with a hoe—an ordinary garden hoe will do—and a square spade, with which to pull the concrete into place. When the concrete is poured from the truck you must make sure every part of the form is filled. Spading the concrete will eliminate any air pockets and help it settle flat. To get the top of the concrete—between the two sides of the form—level and smooth, use a "strike board", which may be any straight piece of wood longer than the footings are wide. Move the strike board quickly from side to side while at the same time pulling it slowly along the top of the form.

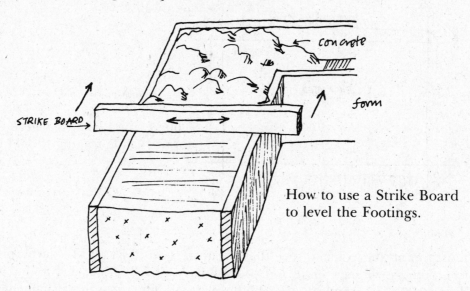

How to use a Strike Board
to level the Footings.

Wash the spade and hoe as soon as you have finished using them or the concrete will dry on them and you will have a hard time chipping it off later. As soon as you can walk on the footings without leaving footprints—within a day or so, depending on the dampness of the weather—you are ready to start on the walls. However, it is a good idea to leave the forms on until the walls are up.

4. Building the Foundation Walls.

Local Building Codes may specify the thickness required for Foundation Walls, but generally, for a small house where the foundation is not going to be much over 6' deep you may use concrete blocks of the 8" x 8" x 16" size. They actually measure slightly less, as shown below.

A standard 3 core (hole) 8" x 8" x 16" block.

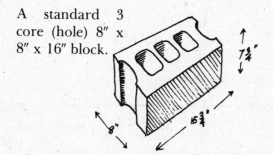

A 2 core corner block. The measurements are the same. Most blocks are now made with 2 cores instead of 3.

Concrete blocks are made from Portland Cement, water and various aggregates such as sand, gravel, cinders or processed slag. They come in many different shapes and sizes, but you will only need the two kinds shown. Whether you get the 2 core type or the 3 core type makes little difference, but you should notice that the "webs" are thicker on one side than the other, and in laying, it is the thick-webbed side which should be up—the better to receive the mortar.

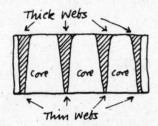

Cross-section of a 3 core block.
(Right way up for laying.)

The blocks are cemented together with mortar, the "recipe" for which is 1 part masonry cement to 3 parts dry sand. Mix the cement and sand thoroughly and then slowly add water until the mix is about the consistency of stiff oatmeal. If you have made it too wet it will run all over the place and you must continue to add commensurate amounts of sand and cement. If you have not added enough water it will be too stiff, and will crumble and not stick to the block.

Cement comes in 94 lb. bags which each contain approximately 1 cubic foot. Sand is measured by the cubic yard, and must be dry, clean mason's sand.
To estimate what you will need for your foundation use the following table.

For every 100 square feet of wall, using 8" x 8" x 16" block	BLOCK	MORTAR	CEMENT	SAND
	110	3¼ cu. ft.	3 bags	¼ cu. yd.

In ordering materials allow at least 10% for waste and remember that a lot depends on how neat and skillful you are.

The depth of the foundation below grade has already been determined by the Frost Line. Bear in mind that the top of the foundation wall should rise two courses or so above grade and you will be able to figure out the area of the wall and the amount of block, sand and cement needed. There is, of course, no reason why you may not make the foundation deeper than the frost line requires if you should need to for any reason—for example if you are planning on installing a furnace which requires more headroom.

The easiest way to make mortar is with a small cement mixer run by a gasoline engine or electricity. It is also possible to do it by hand, although this represents a lot of work even if your foundation is as small as 16' x 20', so rent or borrow one if at all possible. The local lumberyard will tell you where. You must have water now too, so if there is no stream or neighbor nearby, and you haven't yet had a well dug, you must bring it in yourself—by hand, truck or whatever.

Order the materials from either the lumberyard or the Ready-Mix Concrete firm and try and have the block delivered in the middle of the site so that it will be equidistant from all points where it will be needed and you will save yourself a lot of heavy carrying. Have the sand and cement left outside the foundation area near the water supply. Make some provision for keeping the cement dry in case of rain, such as covering it with plastic which may be bought in long rolls from lumberyards. Sweep the top of the footings clean and you are ready to begin laying block.

LAYING THE BLOCK

1. Method

1. Use the plumb bob to locate the corners of the foundation wall on the footing.

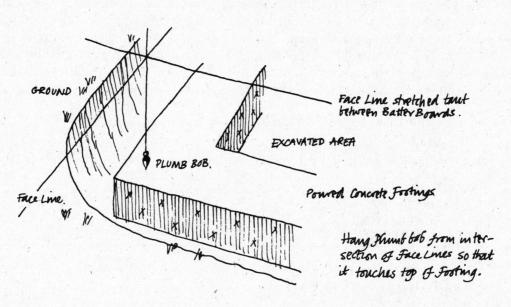

2. Lay out the block around the entire foundation (without mortar), shifting the blocks one way or another so that they will fit between the corners you have marked, leaving about ⅜″ to ½″ for the mortar between each block. This is called CHASING THE BOND. When you have got everything to fit make chalk marks on the footing where the joints come.

The right tool for cutting block is the Brick Hammer, but the Carpenter's Hammer may be substituted.

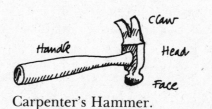

Carpenter's Hammer.

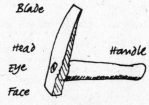

Brick Hammer.

It rarely works out exactly, so you will probably have to cut a block or two to get everything to fit. The block may be easily cut to size by first carefully scoring it all around with the blade of your hammer where you want to cut it, and then hitting the part to be broken off sharply with the face of the hammer.

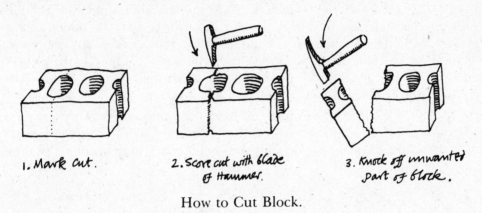

1. Mark cut. 2. Score cut with blade of Hammer. 3. Knock off unwanted part of block.

How to Cut Block.

3. First, lay up three or four courses at the corners. Use plumb bob and level to keep corners straight and plumb.

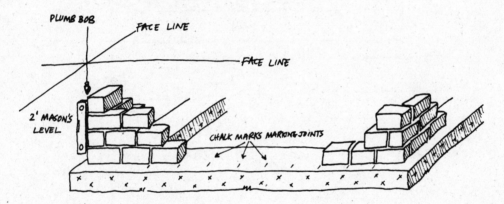

PLUMB BOB
FACE LINE
FACE LINE
2' MASON'S LEVEL
CHALK MARKS MARKING JOINTS

4. After the corners have been built up, fill in the sides, using the chalk marks to position the blocks. Use cut nails to secure the line as they will not turn in the soft mortar joints. (Also useful are several different patent line-holders available at hardware stores.)

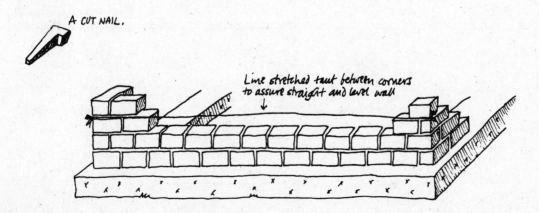

A CUT NAIL.

Line stretched taut between corners to assure straight and level wall

2. Application

The mortar joints should be between ⅜″ and ½″ thick. Sometimes you will have to make them a little thicker or a little thinner in order to have the blocks come out right. The joints should always be staggered—that is, never one joint directly above another. Mortar should be laid only on the outside edges of the block since this method forms an air space in the center which helps to keep the wall dry. Remember to lay the block with the thick webs uppermost.

The only tools you need are a mortar board—somewhere to put the mortar (a wheelbarrow will do, or a flat board on the ground), a pointed trowel with which to apply the mortar, and a mason's level to keep everything straight, plumb and level.

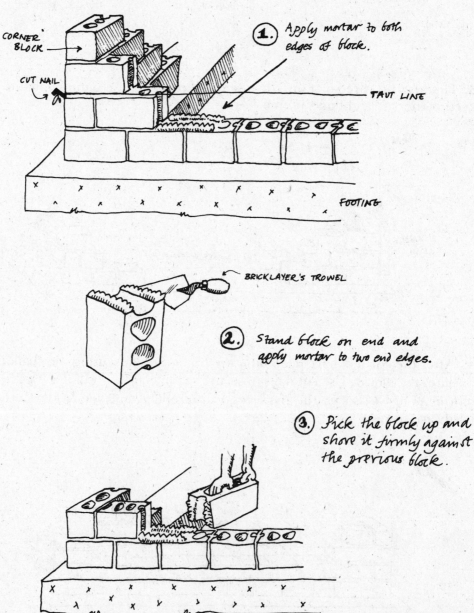

The mortar which is squeezed out between the blocks is cut off with the trowel and placed on the next block, or thrown back on the mortar board. Lay the block so that it just touches the guide line, tap it with the handle of the trowel to sit it straight and check it lengthways, crossways, and diagonally with the level.

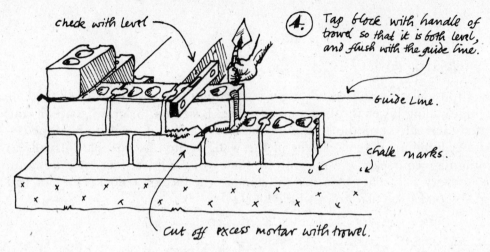

check with level

4. Tap block with handle of trowel so that it is both level, and flush with the guide line.

Guide Line.

chalk marks.

cut off excess mortar with trowel.

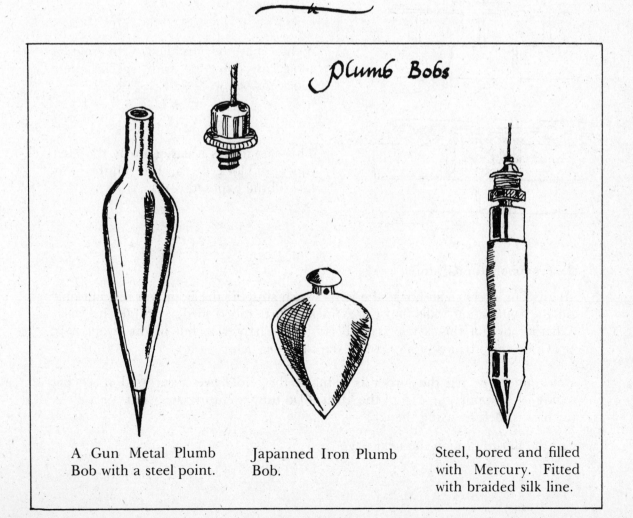

Plumb Bobs

A Gun Metal Plumb Bob with a steel point.

Japanned Iron Plumb Bob.

Steel, bored and filled with Mercury. Fitted with braided silk line.

There remain but four more operations before the foundation is complete.

1. Ventilation.	**3.** Anchor Bolts.
2. Provision for Girders.	**4.** Waterproofing.

1. Ventilation.

If the foundation you are building is big enough to stand up in it is called a basement; anything lower is called a crawl space. Basement or crawl space, it must be vented to avoid rot on the bottom of the house. All that needs to be done is to insert an aluminum screened vent in the wall, as high as possible—usually in the penultimate course, at the rate of one for every 50 lineal feet, or a minimum of one in every wall. They measure the same as the face of a block, i.e., 8″ x 16″, and so merely take the place of a whole block.

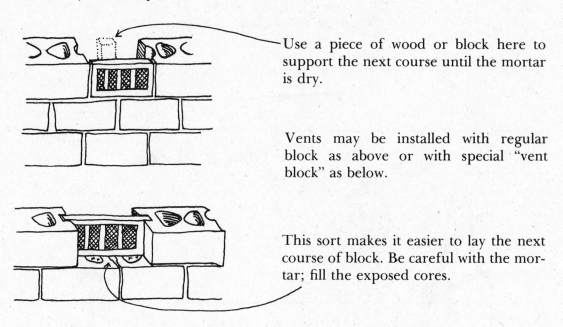

Use a piece of wood or block here to support the next course until the mortar is dry.

Vents may be installed with regular block as above or with special "vent block" as below.

This sort makes it easier to lay the next course of block. Be careful with the mortar; fill the exposed cores.

2. Provision for Girders.

In any but a *very* small house the joists which support the floor will rest not only on the foundation walls, but on extra supports called girders inside the walls. Whether or not this is necessary belongs to Chapter 2, but in the event it is, provision must be made now, while the walls are being built.

Determine how big the girder is going to be and leave a recessed space big enough to support the end of the girder. Do this by cutting away part of a block (or blocks) before laying them.

See the illustration on the next page.

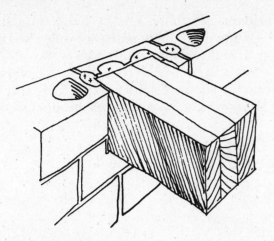

A Girder made from three 2″ x 10″'s resting on wall with part of the block cut out to receive it.

3. Anchor Bolts.

When you arrive at the top and last course you must set **ANCHOR BOLTS** into the block. These are long bolts which are cemented into the cores every 4 or 5 feet and which are placed so that they protrude in order that the "sills" may be bolted to them when the framing is begun. For this is how the house is attached to the foundation.

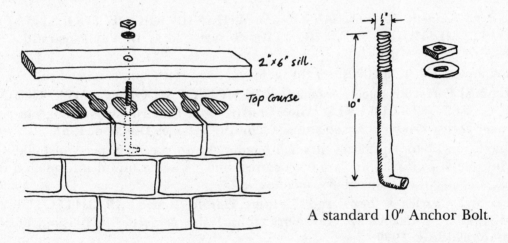

A standard 10″ Anchor Bolt.

When the anchor bolts are set all the cores of the top course should be filled with mortar and smoothed level. Take care to set the bolts as straight as possible—it will make it easier to fit the sill over them. Make sure they stick up at least the thickness of the sill you are going to use so that you can get the washer and nut on.

4. Waterproofing.

When all the walls are built, vents installed, provision for girders made as required, anchor bolts set and the top course filled and levelled, the outside wall should be given a good thick coat of "Foundation Coating" which comes in 5 gallon drums from lumberyards. This is not complete protection but it helps and is certainly worthwhile.

In building a house it is seldom possible to do things one at a time in a strict order. Many things will—and should—happen simultaneously, so while this completes the foundation proper there remain a few operations which may also be done at this time, such as the excavation of drainage ditches, the installation of septic tanks and underground services for water, electricity and fuel, and the back-filling of the foundation, etc., all of which, however, will be discussed in Chapter 6.

BIBLIOGRAPHY

Bailey, Kenneth Holmes. MASONRY: A HANDBOOK OF TOOLS, MATERIALS, METHODS, AND DIRECTIONS. New York: D. Van Nostrand Co., 1945

A complete course in all aspects of masonry, from foundations to stucco.

National Forest Products Association. DESIGN OF WOOD FORMWORK FOR CONCRETE STRUCTURES. Wood Construction Data No. 3. Washington: National Forest Products Association, Technical Services Division, 1961

One of an up-to-date series of small handbooks on specific aspects of building. This one is primarily for large structures, but has some useful information on how to make forms and pour concrete.

Ramsey, Charles George, and Sleeper, Harold Reeve. ARCHITECTURAL GRAPHIC STANDARDS. New York: John Wiley & Sons, 6th Edition, Editor Joseph N. Boaz, 1970

This book is an invaluable source for ANY technical detail you may wonder about, from the load that certain size timbers will support to the amount of space necessary for a built-in telephone. In fact, it is considered a standard item in all architects', builders', and designers' offices.

Ulrey, Harry F. CARPENTERS AND BUILDERS LIBRARY. Vols. I–IV. Indianapolis: Howard W. Sams & Co., 1970

These four volumes, formerly known as Audel's Guides, are a set of books covering most aspects of building, with much useful basic information. Particularly useful here is volume III—Layouts, Foundations, Framing.

CHAPTER TWO. Framing

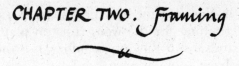

This Chapter is divided into four main parts:

1. Framing Styles, Lumber, Nails & Tools.
2. Framing the Floor.
3. Framing the Walls.
4. Framing the Roof.

1. Framing Styles, Lumber, Nails and Tools.

a. Framing Styles.

Wood is becoming scarcer, the demand is increasing, and consequently the price is rising and the choice diminishing. Time was when only hardwoods were used in the framing of a house—big beams of oak, maple, and chestnut, with mahogany and walnut used for the trim. All these woods are now so expensive that they are used more and more only for furniture and really fine work. Nowadays houses are commonly framed out with softer woods (which our grandfathers used for firewood) such as pine, hemlock, spruce, and fir. Because the available wood has changed, techniques have changed—and sometimes, of course, vice versa. Instead of heavy wooden skeletons such as old barns have, wooden houses now employ a much lighter framework consisting chiefly of pieces of wood no bigger than 2″ x 4″.

There are different methods of constructing such light frameworks, such as **BALLOON FRAME CONSTRUCTION** where the 2″ x 4″ 's, known as studs, which comprise the walls, extend in one piece from foundation to roof; and **BRACED FRAME CONSTRUCTION** which is an adaptation of an old English method using heavy corner posts, sills, and plates with small 2″ x 4″ studs in between.

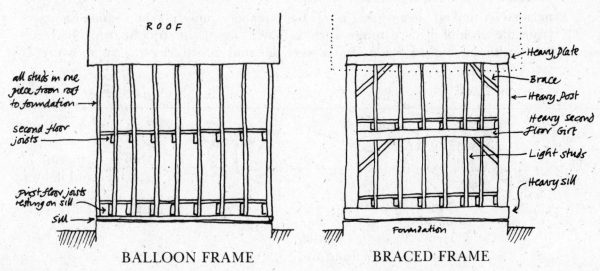

BALLOON FRAME **BRACED FRAME**

A third type, explained in this chapter, is called **WESTERN FRAMING.** What makes this different is that the framing for the walls rests on platforms independently framed, i.e. neither the studs, as in Balloon Framing, nor the posts, as in Braced Framing, are continuous from foundation to roof.

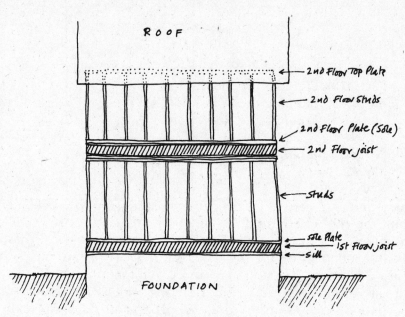

A Two Storied Western Framed House.

b. Lumber.

The wood for framing may be bought directly from a sawmill—in which case it is likely to be "green", i.e. unseasoned and undried, but full dimensional and cheaper; or it may be bought from a lumberyard or building supply company, in which case it is almost sure to be "dry", i.e. seasoned and/or kiln-dried, but "dressed" and more expensive.

DRESSED or "milled" means that it has been planed smooth. When lumber comes from the sawmill it has a rough surface, having been cut straight from the tree trunk with one big saw blade—but a piece of wood called "2″ x 4″ " will measure a

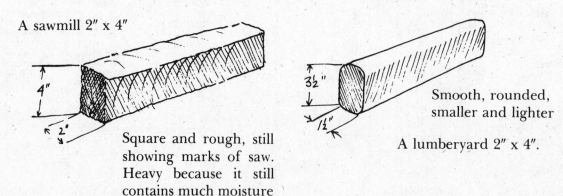

A sawmill 2″ x 4″

Square and rough, still showing marks of saw. Heavy because it still contains much moisture

Smooth, rounded, smaller and lighter

A lumberyard 2″ x 4″.

full two inches by four inches. Dressed lumber, which has been planed on all four sides, measures less than the "nominal" size.

Whether you use sawmill "roughcut" or lumberyard "dressed" is up to you. The difference is basically that roughcut is cheaper and dressed lumber more convenient. The most common sizes needed for framing are kept by all sawmills and lumberyards. They are listed below, showing nominal and actual sizes.

NOMINAL SIZE Sawmills	ACTUAL SIZE Lumberyards
2″ x 4″	1½″ x 3½″
2″ x 6″	1½″ x 5½″
2″ x 8″	1½″ x 7⅜″
2″ x 10″	1½″ x 9⅜″
2″ x 12″	1½″ x 11⅜″

Lumber is sold either by the "Linear" Foot or by the "Board" Foot.

LINEAR FEET is simply the length of any given piece. Therefore 30 Linear Feet of 2″ x 4″ is enough 2″ x 4″ to stretch 30 feet. For example, 3 pieces each 10′ long, or 6 pieces each 5′ long.

BOARD FEET is a way of computing the amount of wood in terms of **UNITS** 1 inch thick, 1 foot wide, and 1 foot long.

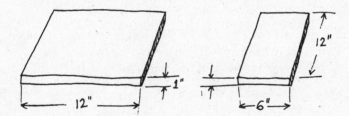

One Board Foot of Wood.   Half a Board Foot of Wood.

To convert wood of any size other than 1″ x 12″ into Board Feet simply multiply the thickness by the width by the length and divide the total by 144 if all the above dimensions are expressed in inches, or by 12 if one of the dimensions is expressed in feet.

E.g. A piece of wood 2″ thick by 6″ wide and 10′ long.

$$\frac{2″ \times 6″ \times 10′}{12} = \frac{120}{12} = 10 \text{ Board Feet.}$$

$$\text{or } \frac{2″ \times 6″ \times 120″}{144} = \frac{1440}{144} = 10 \text{ Board Feet.}$$

Wood is commonly graded at lumberyards according to how full or clear it is of knots. There are numerous classifications but for all practical purposes only "Number One" and "Number Two" need be considered. Number One is generally free of knots, and Number Two is not!

Framing lumber, such as 2″ x 4″, is generally No. 2—tight knots, sound and usable without waste.

c. Nails

For framing a small house * buy one box each of 10d. Common, 16d. Common, and 20d. **COMMON NAILS.** The "d." stands for penny and indicates the size. It used to be—long ago in England—that 100 10d. nails cost 10 pence, 100 16d. nails cost 16 pence, and so on. The "d." being the old English abbreviation for penny. That time is long ago, but the nomenclature remains, even though nails are now bought by the pound rather than the hundred. "Common" indicates the type—a round, wire nail with a flat head. A box holds 50 lbs.

* up to 1,000 square feet

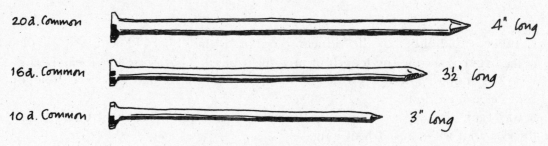

20d. Common   4″ long

16d. Common   3½″ long

10d. Common   3″ long

Common Nails—Actual Size.

Common nails are made in sizes from 2d. (1″ long) to 60d. (6″ long). They are also made with a galvanized coating—to prevent rust where they will remain exposed. There are many other types of nails, such as Finish, Casing, Box, Roofing etc., which will be discussed as they need to be used.

d. Tools.

Here follows an illustrated list of the tools needed for framing. The circular saw and electric drill assume that there is electricity at the site already. This is not indispensable but VERY labor saving.

Buy and use only the BEST—they work better and last longer. Many times you will be able to find second-hand tools in antique stores which are both cheaper and better made than new tools.

Take care of tools—protect sharp edges and sharpen them often. Keep moving parts oiled. Do not allow tools to get wet and rusty.

There are many specialized types of almost every tool illustrated here, some of which will be discussed when necessary—for framing purposes use types similar to those illustrated.

1. A RETRACTABLE METAL TAPE.

10', 12', 16' or even 20' Long.

for measuring.

2. A PENCIL   for marking.

3. A WINDABLE CHALK LINE
for marking long straight lines.

4. A CARPENTER'S METAL FRAMING SQUARE

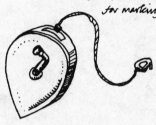

Tongue

Body

This is probably the most complicated tool. Whole books have been written about it. It measures all kinds of angles for rafters, etc., and usually has lots of tables on it. Use it as a big right angle square. The body and the tongue may be 24" and 18", both graduated in inches.

5. A TRY SQUARE

for marking right angles and testing the squareness of wood.

6. A COMBINED TRY & MITER SQUARE

this tool also marks 45° angles.

7. A BEVEL

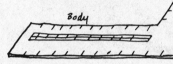

this can be adjusted to mark ANY angle on a piece of wood.

8. A SPIRIT LEVEL

for measuring the plumbness and the levelness of various surfaces.

9. A PLUMB BOB

for measuring plumbness, for marking a spot immediately below something else.

10. A PORTABLE ELECTRIC
CIRCULAR SAW.

for all kinds of sawing.

11. A HAND SAW

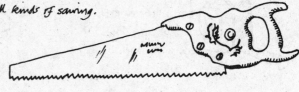

13. A 5lb. MAUL a kind of lightweight, portable sledge-hammer.

12. A CARPENTER'S CLAW HAMMER

12 oz., 14 oz., 16 oz. or even 20 oz.! the heavier the hammer the quicker it will drive a nail — but the stronger you must be!

14. A CAT'S PAW

for removing nails from tight corners.

15. AN ELECTRIC DRILL
for making holes.

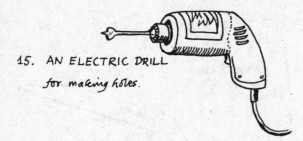

16. A 2' WRECKING BAR

for prying things loose & pulling nails.

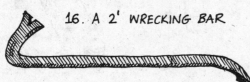

18. A 3/4" PLASTIC HANDLED
WOOD CHISEL

an all-purpose chisel you may hit with a hammer.

17. A JACK PLANE

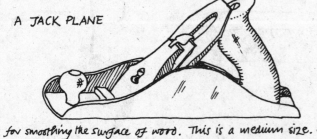

for smoothing the surface of wood. This is a medium size.

19. A SCREWDRIVER
for screws.

2. Framing the Floor.

The framed floor or "platform" of a Western Framed house consists of:

1. Girders.
2. Sills.
3. Joists.
4. Sub floor.

1. Girders.

If the side walls of your house are more than 16′ apart, i.e. your house is more than 16′ wide, it will be best to install a girder. A girder is a beam which runs the *length* of the house, and which acts as an additional support for the floor beams—called "joists."

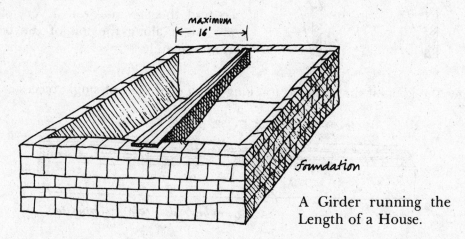

A Girder running the Length of a House.

The girder should be set at least 4″ into the foundation wall. The top of the girder must be "flush" with the top of the sill since the same joists which are going to rest on the sill must also rest on the girder at the same level.

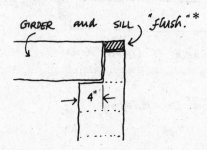

Showing how Girder sits in Foundation Wall.

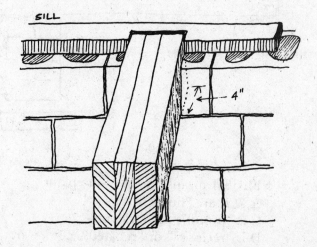

* See next page for explanation of "flush."

Girders are usually made from 3 pieces of 2″ x 12″ nailed together with 16d. nails. Choose the flattest piece for the center, and if the wood is not perfectly straight make the girder with the "Crown" up. This will counter the weight carried and there will be no sag.

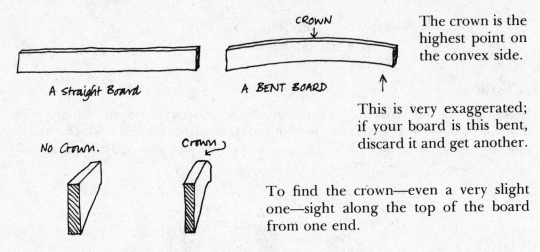

The crown is the highest point on the convex side.

This is very exaggerated; if your board is this bent, discard it and get another.

To find the crown—even a very slight one—sight along the top of the board from one end.

Stagger the joints if the girder is too long to be made out of single pieces.

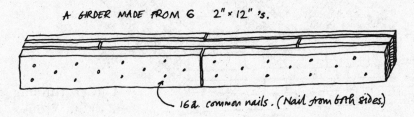

If the Girder is more than 20′ long it should be supported at its center by some kind of pillar, or pier—like the one shown below.

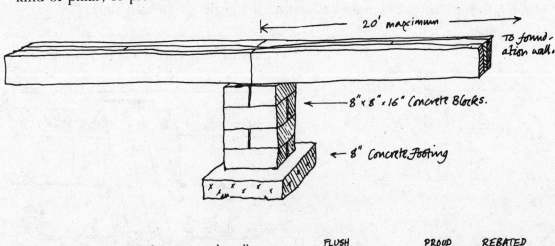

* FLUSH means "in the same plane".
  A & B are "flush".
  C is "proud", i.e. sticks up.
  D is "recessed" or "rebated", i.e. lower.

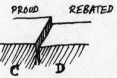

Ascertain the length the girder must be—by measuring the distance from one recessed end of the foundation to the other—("x" in the diagram), and make up the girder from 2″ x 12″'s on top of one of the side walls. When it is made just roll it over and into place.

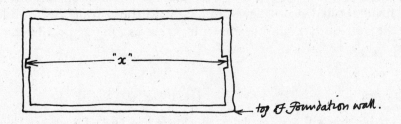

If a center support is necessary it should be built as nearly level with the top of the walls as possible. It is better to build it slightly lower rather than slightly higher since the girder can always be shimmed up if it is not level. In fact a slight crown (of about 1″) is often given to the girder to obviate any settling of the center support.

2. Sills.

The Sill is the timber which runs all around the top of the foundation wall—and is in fact bolted to it—to which the joists, and indirectly the whole superstructure, are nailed. It is thus the link between the foundation and the house on top, and as such it is the most important piece of wood in the house—and the most costly and difficult piece to repair.

For small houses sills may be made from 2″ x 6″. They should be marked and drilled to fit over the anchor bolts set in the top of the foundation in such a way as to be flush with the outside face of the foundation wall.

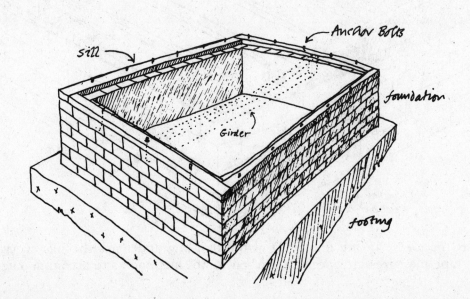

In order to prevent water filling any unevennesses between the sill and the top of the foundation wall, the sill is sometimes laid in a bed of wet mortar, the nuts on the anchor bolts being tightened down after the mortar has dried. An easier way is to lay the sill on a bed of some other rot resistant material such as fiber glass. This may be bought especially for this purpose in long rolls, 6″ or 8″ wide, or you may cut up your own from regular fiber glass insulation. In any event the sills should be firmly bolted down, level and tight to the top of the foundation and flush with the outside face, and made with pieces as long as possible.

3. Joists.

When the girder and sill are in place, the joists are laid. The joists comprise the frame for the floor, and are nailed to the sill and girder. They are commonly made from 2″ x 10″ (although they may be heavier if they have to span longer distances than 16′) and are placed on edge every 16″.

They are trimmed with "headers" at the ends, and every 8′ or less "bridging" is installed to prevent the joists springing sideways under the load. A better form of bridging is "blocking" made from pieces the same size as the joists. Any openings in the floor (for stairs or a trapdoor) require trimmers—which are simply double joists, and headers. All of these terms are illustrated below.

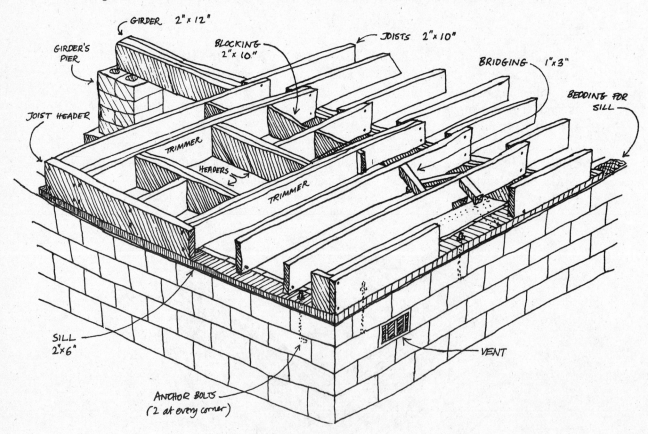

To lay the joists, start at one END of the building and mark the sills every 16″. Most tape measures are specially marked in 16″ increments to accommodate this often used measurement. If you are proceeding from LEFT to RIGHT, as in the diagram below, the joists will sit just to the right of the marks you have made. Do not worry if the distance between the last two marks is less than 16″.

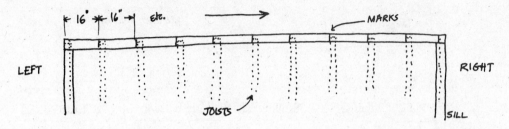

When you have marked the sill, mark the girder the same way—starting from the same end!

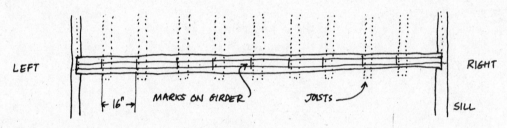

The joists should then be nailed to the sill and the girder in such a way as to leave 1½″ at the sill for the joist header (or box beam as it is sometimes called), and project past the girder at least a couple of inches.

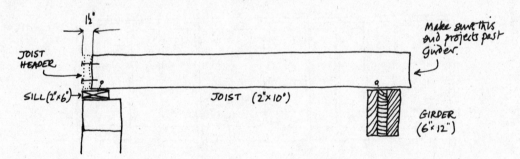

"Toenail" the joist from both sides to the sill at one end and the girder at the other.

TOENAILING with 16d. Common Nails.

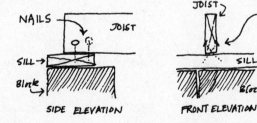

It may help to nail two joists to the sill, the distance of one header's length apart first, nail the header to these two joists, and then install the intervening joists, butting them firmly against the header.

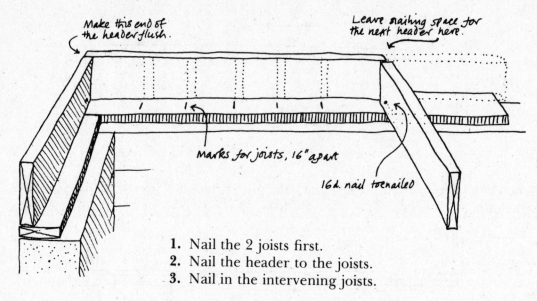

1. Nail the 2 joists first.
2. Nail the header to the joists.
3. Nail in the intervening joists.

When all the joists, and headers, are in place on this side of the house, do the same thing on the other side, EXCEPT that the first joist will meet the first joist from the other side head-on and the second joist should be 14½″ away, not 16″, so that it will be next to the second joist from the other side as shown.

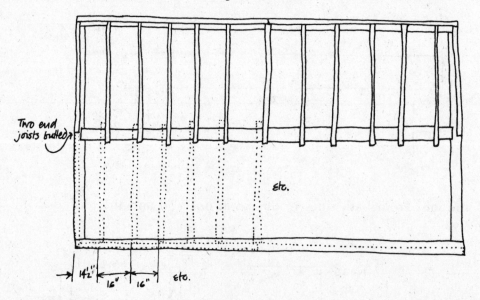

Nail the joists where they overlap at the center.

There must be some way into the basement or crawl space, so choose a good spot which is not going to be under a partition wall or a bathtub and plan an opening. By leaving out one joist the opening will be wide enough. Double the joists on either side of the opening—they then become known as "trimmers"—and toenail in double headers as shown. Finally, install the remainder of the intervening joists.

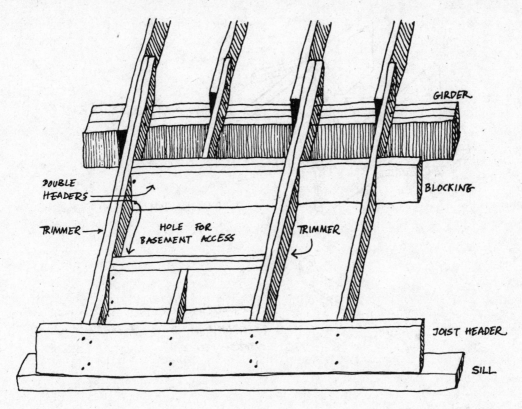

If the joists span 8′ or more (the span is the distance *between* supports) install a row of blocking. Block the ends of the joists over the girder as well.

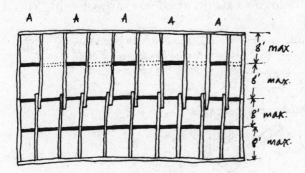

Cut the blocking $1/16''$ longer than the space between two joists and insert every other one first—as at "A". Then fill in the other ones, keeping the line straight. This method keeps the strain evenly distributed and the joists straight.

Plan of Floor Frame Showing
Blocking.
(Blocking shown as solid lines)

Cross Bridging is often used instead of Solid Bridging (Blocking)—it makes the electrician's job of threading the wires about under the floor much easier, but blocking should be used under partitions and under heavy loads. Cross bridging may be made from 1″ x 3″, although 1″ x 4″ is better. When installing it nail only the top ends—wait until the flooring is laid before nailing the lower ends.

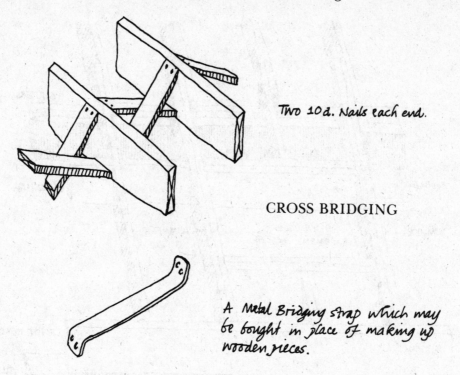

Two 10d. Nails each end.

CROSS BRIDGING

A Metal Bridging strap which may be bought in place of making up wooden pieces.

4. The Sub Floor.

The Sub Floor is a kind of platform covering the entire length and breadth of the building. It may be made from boards 1″ x 4″, 1″ x 6″, or 1″ x 8″. These boards are laid diagonally. Or, it may be made from a grade of plywood known as plyscord, and should be at least ½″ thick.

Start in one corner and cover the entire area—except, of course, any opening you

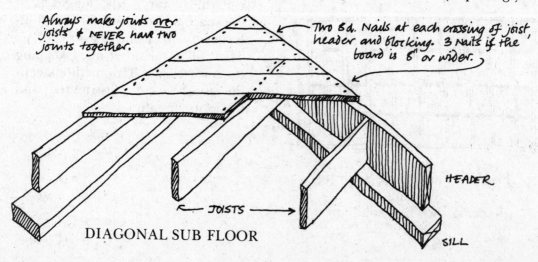

Always make joints over joists & NEVER have two joints together.

Two 8d. Nails at each crossing of joist, header and blocking. 3 Nails if the board is 8″ or wider.

HEADER

JOISTS

DIAGONAL SUB FLOOR

SILL

may have made. Cut the boards off at a 45° angle (using the combined try and miter square) and always join them on a joist. Use two nails per joist (3, if the board is 8″ or more wide). The ends may be allowed to hang over the edge of the building until the whole area is floored, when they can all be cut off at once. This type of floor is very strong and helps prevent squeaks when the finished floor is later laid.

Plyscord is quicker to lay but may well be more expensive. It comes in 4′ x 8′ sheets and should be laid with the 4′ side resting on a joist. The 4′ sides should never line up; cut one board in half to avoid this, as in the diagram.

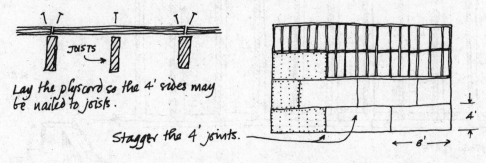

PLAN OF PLYWOOD SUBFLOOR

If you are going to use plyscord it is often worthwhile to study the layout of the area to be covered in order to see if with a little ingenuity the sheets may be laid in such a way as to utilize the joists, headers, and blocking as nailing surfaces and leave a minimum of edges unsupported and to make necessary the cutting of as few sheets as possible.

The plywood is nailed every 10″ or so using "Plywood Underlayment Nails", which are made with rings on the shank so they won't pull out so easily.

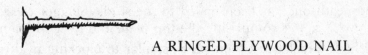

A RINGED PLYWOOD NAIL

Make every effort to keep the sheets of plywood square with the building and as tight to one another as possible.

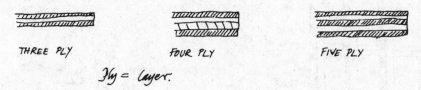

THREE PLY   FOUR PLY   FIVE PLY

1 ply = layer.

3. Framing the Walls.

With the sub floor down, and armed with a floor plan showing the location and dimensions of windows, doors and interior walls (partitions), framing of the walls may begin.

Every house of different design presents its own problems of framing construction, and more particularly, the order in which things should be done. Experience is the best teacher but if the fundamental techniques are understood, a little forethought and common sense will clear away many difficulties.

What follows is a series of illustrations showing how the various details for corners, windows, doors, and partitions etc. are formed.

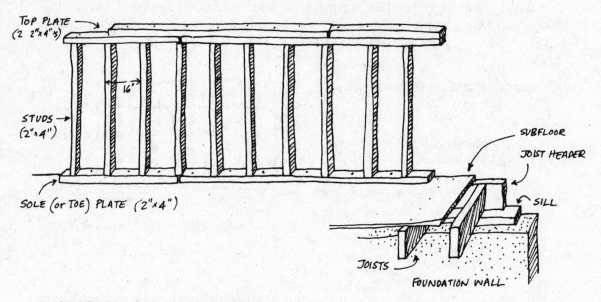

1. SECTION OF WALL FRAMING.

1. Sole plate nailed through subfloor to joist with 16d. Common Nails, 16″ o.c. (= on center—every 16″).

2. Studs nailed to Sole Plate 16″ o.c. with 10d. Common Nails. Two nails per stud.

3. Top plate nailed to studs 16″ o.c., same nailing.

4. Top plate made of TWO 2″ x 4″'s, the top one nailed to the underneath one *after* the underneath one has been nailed to the studs. Stagger the joints, i.e. do not have the two 2″ x 4″'s comprising the top plate end over the same stud.

5. Cats are 2″ x 4″'s nailed between studs, similar to blocking in the joists. They help stiffen the wall and provide extra nailing surface.

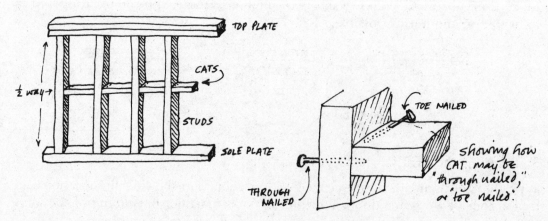

2. CORNERS.

"A" and "B" are methods which may be used if rough-sawn full dimensional 2″ x 4″'s are used.

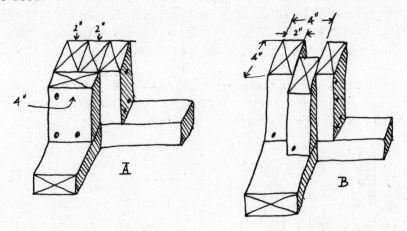

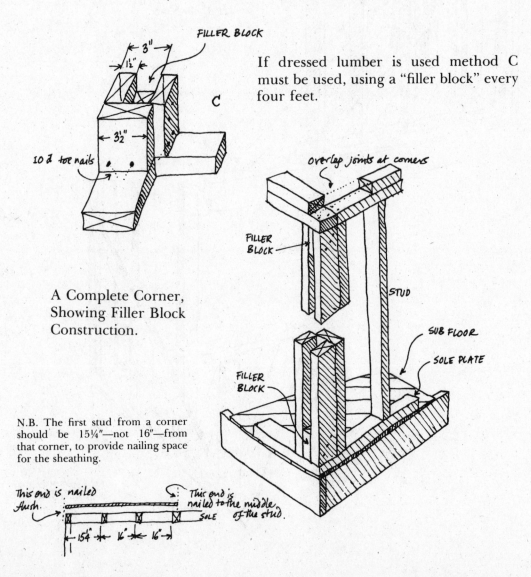

FILLER BLOCK

C

If dressed lumber is used method C must be used, using a "filler block" every four feet.

3″
1½″

3½″

10 d toe nails

overlap joints at corners

FILLER BLOCK

STUD

A Complete Corner, Showing Filler Block Construction.

SUB FLOOR

SOLE PLATE

FILLER BLOCK

N.B. The first stud from a corner should be 15¼″—not 16″—from that corner, to provide nailing space for the sheathing.

This end is nailed flush.

This end is nailed to the middle of the stud.

SOLE

15¼″   16″   16″

3. CORNER BRACING.

Corner bracing is often dispensed with, especially if plywood sheathing is used on the outside, but it is well worth the effort if you live in an area of high winds. In any case in many areas the local building code makes it mandatory. There are two ways of bracing; one is with 2″ x 4″ 's forming a triangle with the studs in every corner, and the other is letting a 1″ x 4″ into the outside face of the studs, also at an angle.

Ideally, Corner bracing should extend from the top plate to the sole plate at an angle of 45°. This is rarely possible because of windows and doors, etc. But the closer you can get to this, the stronger it will be.

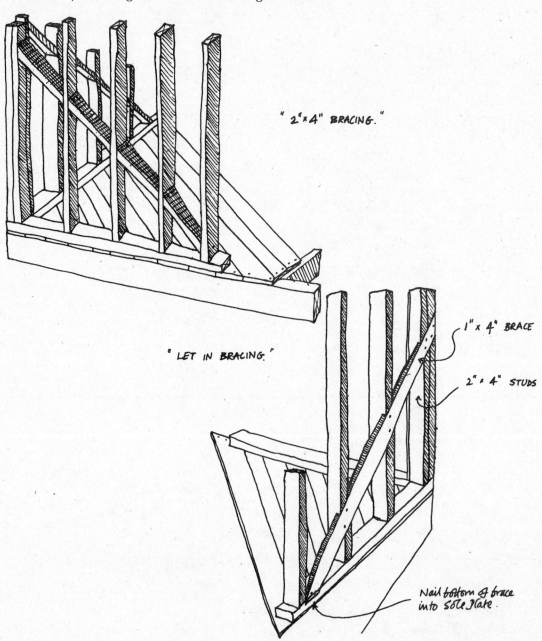

" 2"x 4" BRACING. "

" LET IN BRACING. "

1" x 4" BRACE

2" x 4" STUDS

Nail bottom of brace into sole plate.

4. WINDOW OPENINGS.

All studding at openings must be double to provide adequate nailing for the trim.

Extra care should be taken to make the openings as square as possible—this will make the installation of the windows much easier.

If the opening is wider than 3′ the headers should be 2″ x 6″ 's; under 3′ you may use 2″ x 4″ 's.

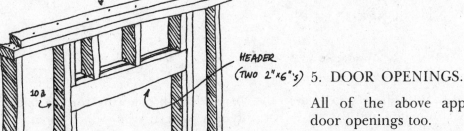

TOP PLATE (Top 2″ x 4″ removed to show nailing.)

HEADER, TWO 2″ 6″ 's

DOUBLE STUD

ROUGH SILL TWO 2″ x 4″ 's

Nailing (10 d.)

JACK STUDS

DIAGONAL SUB FLOOR

JOISTS

JOIST HEADER

Make the opening at least 3″ larger all round than the window to go in it. If in doubt make it bigger since you can always add another stud if it is too big.

TOP PLATE

HEADER (TWO 2″x6″'s)

10 d

CAT

DOUBLE STUD

10d T.N.

SOLE PLATE

10 d

INSIDE STUDS TO FLOOR

5. DOOR OPENINGS.

All of the above applies to door openings too.

The width of the rough opening depends on the method used to trim the door. Remember it has to be as wide as the door, plus the width of both jambs, plus ½″ or so for fitting.

If the lumber used is dressed, a ½″ piece of plywood inserted between the two pieces of the header will make the header the width of the studs.

6. PARTITIONS.

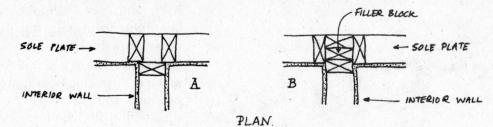

PLAN.

TWO METHODS OF CONNECTING
PARTITION TO OUTSIDE WALL.

Partitions are interior walls which divide the building into rooms and passageways. Try to locate partitions which run parallel with the floor joists over joists. If the partitions are to have any load-carrying function—such as supporting part of the roof—the joists should be doubled up.

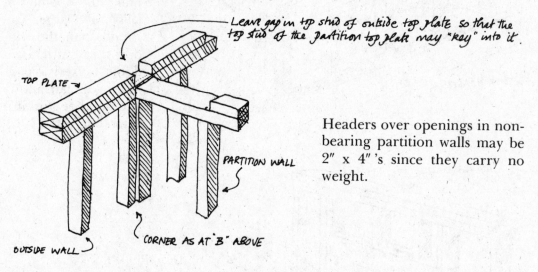

Headers over openings in non-bearing partition walls may be 2" x 4"'s since they carry no weight.

When cutting studs, first cut *one* to the correct length (allowing for the sole plate and the top plate), and then use this stud as a pattern from which to cut all the others.

The easiest way to construct framing is in sections, on the floor. This way the sole plate can be nailed to the studs from underneath. Then the whole section is lifted up and nailed to the subfloor, plumbed with the spirit level and braced.

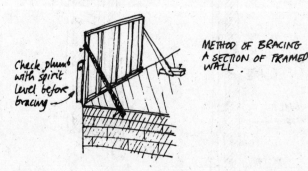

4. Framing the Roof.

The roof is framed out with **RAFTERS**, which are to the roof as the joists are to the floor, and the studs to the wall. There are many different shapes a roof can be, all of which have different names and all of which require differing techniques of construction.

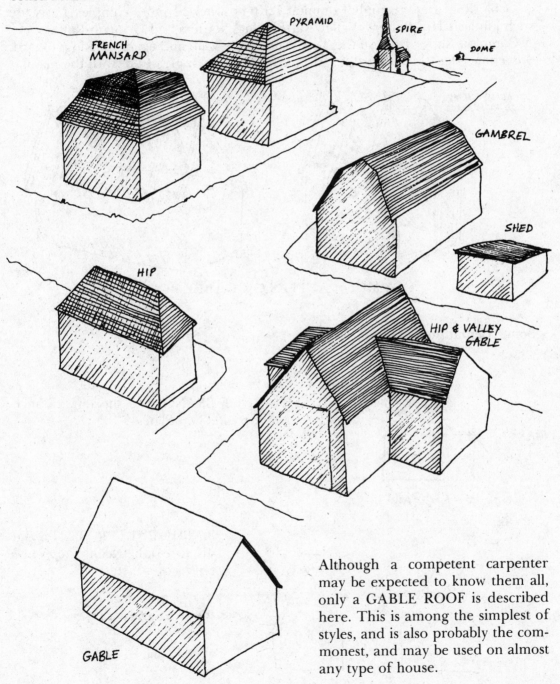

Although a competent carpenter may be expected to know them all, only a GABLE ROOF is described here. This is among the simplest of styles, and is also probably the commonest, and may be used on almost any type of house.

The main purpose of a roof is to keep out rain and snow, and apart from esthetic considerations this is the most important factor in determining the roof's **PITCH**— the steepness of the roof's slope. In areas of heavy snowfall a steeply pitched roof is desirable as it allows the snow to slide off. And yet a layer of snow is extra insulation and sometimes steepness of pitch is tempered with a heavier construction to withstand and support the extra weight. In other areas roofs are actually built to collect the rain!

A Gable Roof requires only Common Rafters, whereas more complex roofs use such kinds as Hip Rafters, Valley Rafters, Jack Rafters and Octagon Rafters, etc. A Common Rafter rests on the Top Plate of the wall, and against a Ridge Board. Sometimes the Ridge Board is left out. It forms an angle of 90° with the plate.

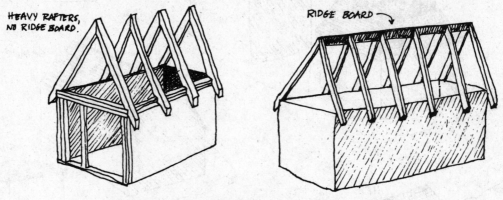

COMMON RAFTERS ON GABLE ROOFS

Some Definitions.

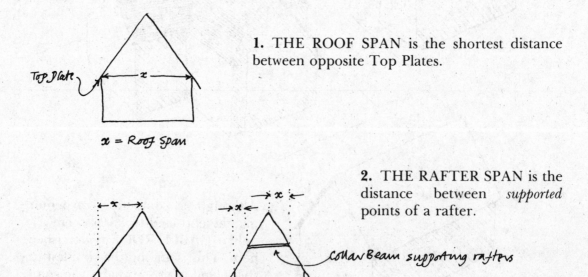

1. THE ROOF SPAN is the shortest distance between opposite Top Plates.

2. THE RAFTER SPAN is the distance between *supported* points of a rafter.

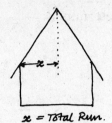

x = Total Run.

3. THE TOTAL RUN is the *level* distance over which a rafter passes—this is usually half the Roof Span.

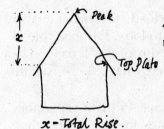

x - Total Rise.

4. THE TOTAL RISE is the vertical distance from the Top Plate to the Peak (the top of the Roof).

5. THE PITCH of a roof is usually expressed in terms of the RISE in inches per foot unit of RUN. It may also be expressed as a fraction, or in degrees.

For example, a roof which rises 6″ for every foot of run has a 6 in 12 pitch. This is also called ¼ pitch.

RISE in inches	RUN in inches	DEGREES	PITCH
3	12	15°	⅛
6	12	26½°	¼
8	12	33½°	⅓
12	12	45°	½
16	12	53°	⅔
18	12	56½°	¾
24	12	63½°	1

ROOF SLOPES IN RUN & RISE, DEGREES AND PITCH.

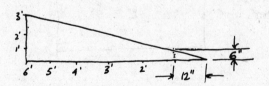

This roof is ¼ Pitch; i.e. 12″ in from the plate it is 6″ higher than the plate.
The Total Run is 6′.
The Total Rise is 3′.
The angle at the plate is 26½°.

Before the roof may be framed the following points must be determined:

1. The Pitch.
2. The Size and Spacing of the Rafters.
3. Length of Rafters.
4. The Cuts.

1. The Pitch.

This is a question of balance between the possible snowload, the heaviness or lightness of construction, and the way you want the house to look. For example, if you live in a heavy snowfall area and you want a low pitched roof it will have to be made of heavier construction than it would be if you lived where there was no snow to be borne.

The easiest pitch to build is ½ pitch because then all cuts are 45°. But remember that ½ pitch, or 12″ in 12″, on a wide building necessitates longer rafters than would a smaller pitched roof.

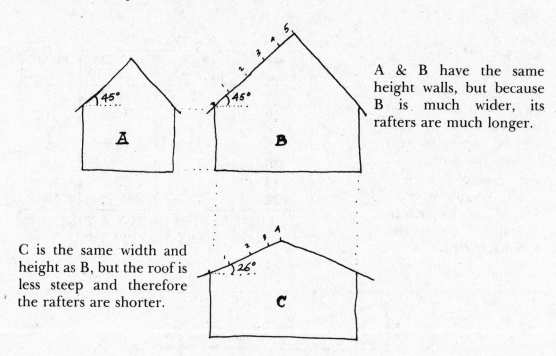

A & B have the same height walls, but because B is much wider, its rafters are much longer.

C is the same width and height as B, but the roof is less steep and therefore the rafters are shorter.

2. The Size and Spacing of the Rafters.

The SIZE of the rafters is a function of the rafter span and the pitch of the roof. This may only be properly computed by reference to tables showing the load bearing capacities and deflection of various woods. For a roof of ½ pitch with a span of around 20′ (rafter span would be 10′), 2″ x 8″ lumber is sufficient for rafters—even when snow must be borne.

Remember though, that the rafter span may be shortened by the addition of a collar beam—a timber from one rafter, horizontally, to the opposite rafter.

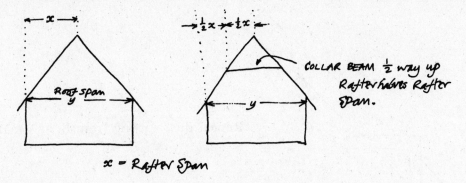

The spacing of rafters is usually 16″ on center (one every 16″). The further apart they are, the more they must each carry, and so the bigger they should be.

3. The Length of Rafters.

The length of the rafter may be found using Pythagoras' Theorem—

$$A^2 + B^2 = C^2$$

where A = the Rafter Span, B = the Total Rise, and C = the Rafter.

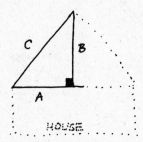

However, few carpenters carry Square Root Tables around with them, and finding square roots leaves room for error. There is a far simpler method, using the framing square. All that is necessary is to know the total run and the total rise— i.e. the pitch.

Let us assume we are going to build the roof with ½ pitch. The total rise is 10′ and the total run is 10′. Lay the rafter on its side and place the framing square (which, whatever else is marked on it, will have all its edges graduated in inches) so that 12″ coincides with the edge of the wood.

This represents 12″ of rise. Call it point A. Swivel the square around so that the other 12″ mark coincides with a point we shall call B. This represents 12″ of run.

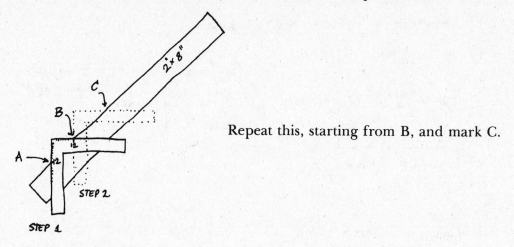

Repeat this, starting from B, and mark C.

If the total run of the rafter had been 2′ you would have now marked off the length—i.e. the distance from A to C. Since the total run is 10′, you must repeat the first step 10 times—once for each 12 inches!

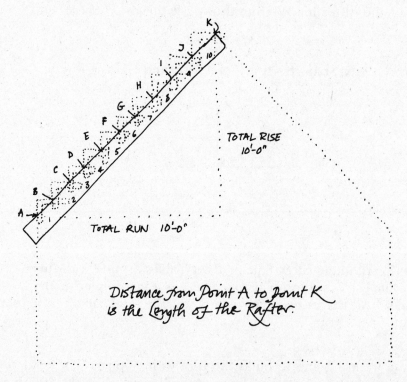

Distance from Point A to Point K is the Length of the Rafter.

**SHOWING ALL THE STEPS IN THE LAYING OUT
OF THE LENGTH OF THE RAFTER**

4. The Cuts.

Rafters must be cut at both ends. Where they meet is called the Top or Plumb Cut. Where they touch the plate is known as the Seat Cut. The part of the rafter which extends past the plate is known (if it exists) as the Tail or Lookout. This may be sawed in different ways depending on whether the Eaves (the overhang of the rafters at the side of the building) are going to be left exposed or whether a cornice is going to be built around them.

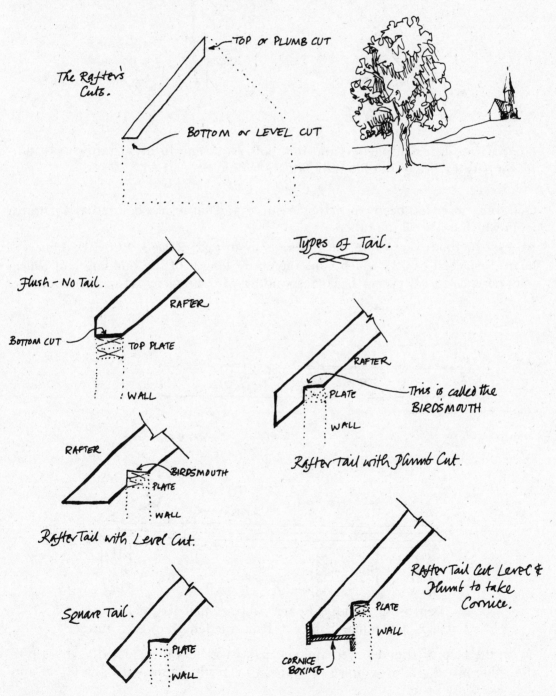

The Rafter's Cuts.

TOP or PLUMB CUT

BOTTOM or LEVEL CUT

Types of Tail.

Flush - No Tail.

RAFTER

BOTTOM CUT — TOP PLATE

WALL

RAFTER

BIRDSMOUTH
PLATE
WALL

Rafter Tail with Level Cut.

RAFTER

PLATE — This is called the BIRDSMOUTH

WALL

Rafter Tail with Plumb Cut.

Square Tail.

PLATE
WALL

Rafter Tail Cut Level & Plumb to take Cornice.

PLATE
WALL

CORNICE BOXING

If the roof is built with a 12″ in 12″ pitch all the rafter cuts may be marked out with a miter square, since all the angles are 45°.

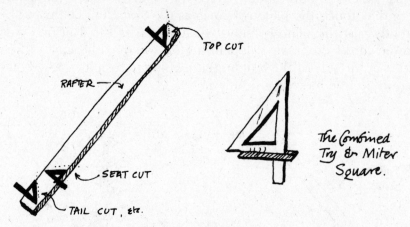

For roofs of different pitches, and for roofs requiring different rafters with different cuts the use of the Framing Square should be learned.*

Once one rafter has been correctly measured and cut it may be used as a pattern from which to cut all the others.

An easy method of erecting the rafters is by using a RIDGE BOARD. This is a board, usually 1″ x 12″, which runs the entire length of the building and which may be marked off every 16″ corresponding with a similar set of marks on the plates.

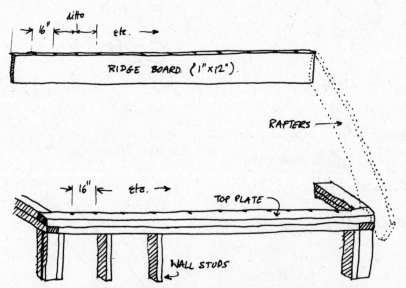

When using a Ridge Board subtract half its thickness (⅜″ if it is a nominal 1″ board) from the length of each rafter.

(With the help of friends) erect the end pair of rafters first, nailed at the top to the ridge board. Hold or brace the rafters perfectly plumb—use the level—and

* See Bibliography.

erect a second pair at the other end of the ridge board. Then all the intervening rafters may be slid up over the plate and nailed in place, to both the Ridge Board and the top plate. In order not to push the Ridge Board out of a straight line erect the rafters in pairs rather than all from one side first and then those from the other side.

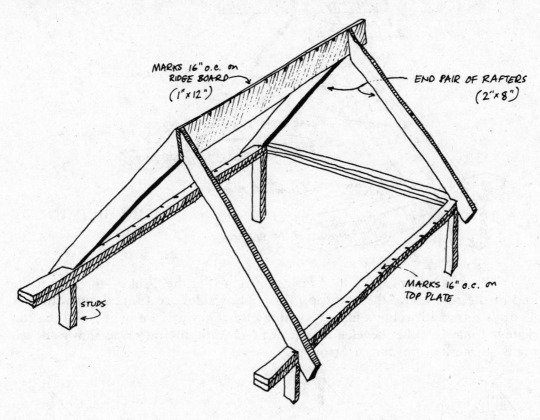

If the building is too long to use a single board for the ridge, it (the Ridge Board) should be joined between two rafters.

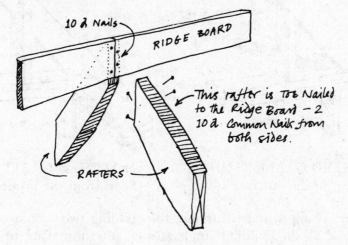

If the rafters are long enough to require Collar Beams (or Ties), they should be the same size as the rafters and nailed to each pair of rafters, level, no further up the rafter than half way.

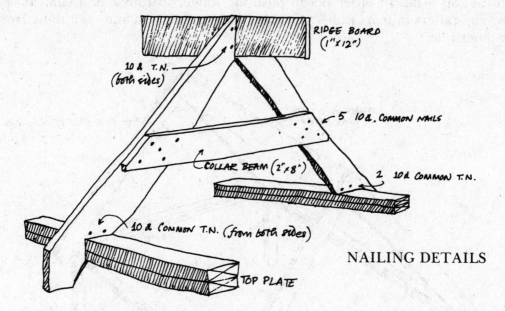

RIDGE BOARD
(1"x12")

10 d. T.N.
(both sides)

5 10 d. COMMON NAILS

COLLAR BEAM (2"x8")

2 10 d COMMON T.N.

10 d COMMON T.N. (from both sides)

TOP PLATE

NAILING DETAILS

When the roof is framed it only remains to frame out the Gables—the area at the end of the roof above the end top plates. The gables are framed out with 2" x 4" studs set on 16" centers like everything else. They are toe nailed into the top plate but may be either beveled under, or notched to, the rafters as shown. Beveling is quicker but notching is stronger.

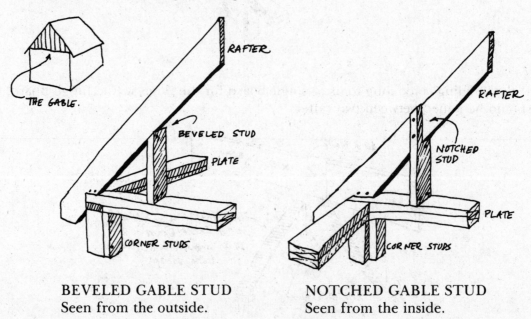

THE GABLE.

RAFTER

BEVELED STUD

PLATE

CORNER STUDS

RAFTER

NOTCHED STUD

PLATE

CORNER STUDS

BEVELED GABLE STUD
Seen from the outside.

NOTCHED GABLE STUD
Seen from the inside.

The procedure, using western framing, for building two or more storied buildings is the same as for building single stories. The top plate of the first floor becomes the sill for the second floor joists and the whole structure is repeated.

For buildings with 3 stories the first floor framing should be heavier, but the principle remains the same.

If there is to be an attic the joists for the attic floor are nailed to the rafters just as are the collar beams, but they rest upon the top plate and are toenailed into it. The second floor joists must span the same distance as the first floor joists. Therefore if a girder was necessary for the first floor, a girder will have to be made for the second floor, seated on studs at the top plate so that the top of the girder is flush with the top of the plate.

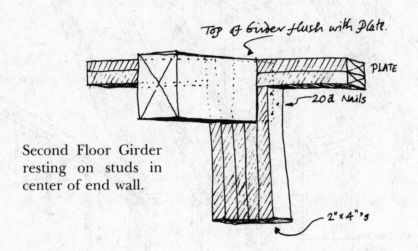

Second Floor Girder resting on studs in center of end wall.

Similarly, if the first floor girder required a support in the middle a post will have to be built under the middle of the second floor girder too.

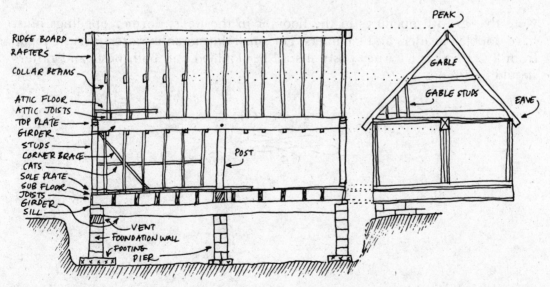

A full discussion of DORMERS (vertical window openings in roofs) is beyond the scope of this volume, for there are almost as many varieties of dormers as there are of roofs. The principles of framing are the same as for other parts of the house.

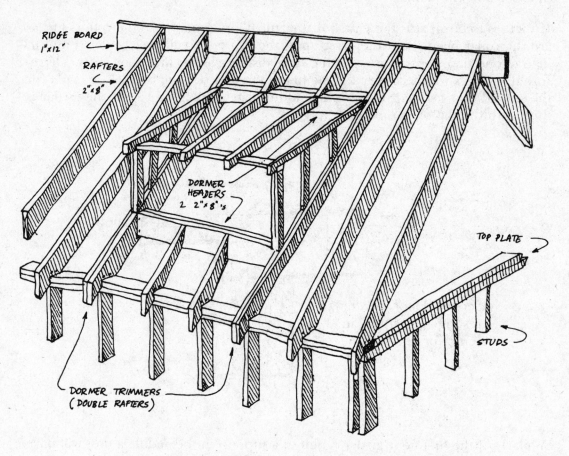

RIDGE BOARD
1"x12"

RAFTERS
2"x8"

DORMER
HEADERS
2 2"x8"'s

TOP PLATE

STUDS

DORMER TRIMMERS
(DOUBLE RAFTERS)

The Framing of a Shed Roof Dormer in a Gable Roof.

Note that as with openings in the floor or in the walls, dormer openings must have doubled headers and trimmers. For small dormers the rafters may be made from 2″ x 4″ 's. The corner posts should be doubled and both posts and rafters should be 16″ o.c.

For buildings with 3 stories the first floor framing should be heavier, but the principle remains the same.

If there is to be an attic the joists for the attic floor are nailed to the rafters just as are the collar beams, but they rest upon the top plate and are toenailed into it. The second floor joists must span the same distance as the first floor joists. Therefore if a girder was necessary for the first floor, a girder will have to be made for the second floor, seated on studs at the top plate so that the top of the girder is flush with the top of the plate.

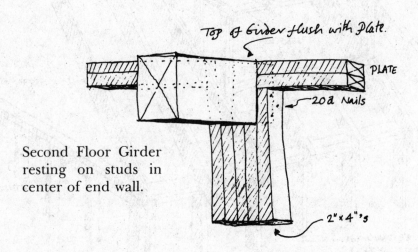

Top of Girder flush with Plate.

PLATE

20 d Nails

Second Floor Girder resting on studs in center of end wall.

2" x 4" 's

Similarly, if the first floor girder required a support in the middle a post will have to be built under the middle of the second floor girder too.

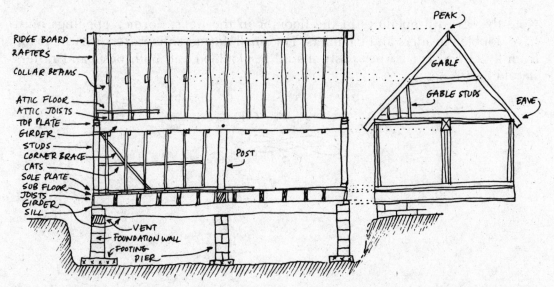

A full discussion of DORMERS (vertical window openings in roofs) is beyond the scope of this volume, for there are almost as many varieties of dormers as there are of roofs. The principles of framing are the same as for other parts of the house.

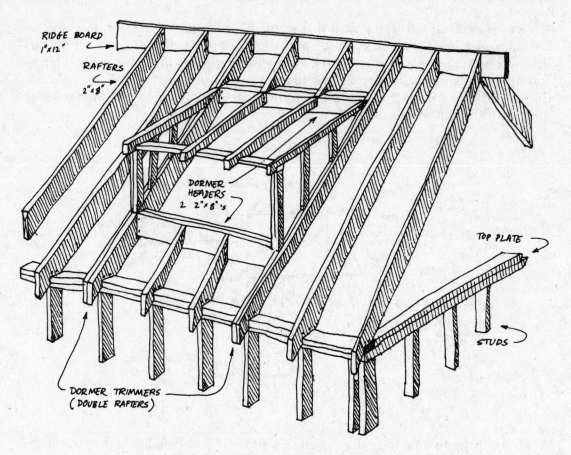

The Framing of a Shed Roof Dormer in a Gable Roof.

Note that as with openings in the floor or in the walls, dormer openings must have doubled headers and trimmers. For small dormers the rafters may be made from 2″ x 4″'s. The corner posts should be doubled and both posts and rafters should be 16″ o.c.

BIBLIOGRAPHY

Anderson, L. O. WOOD-FRAME HOUSE CONSTRUCTION. Agricultural Handbook No. 73. Washington: U.S. Department of Agriculture, 1970 *

A useful government publication. Illustrated orthodox approaches to conventional houses.

Forest Products Laboratory, Forest Research-Forest Service. WOOD HANDBOOK. Washington: U.S. Department of Agriculture, 1940 *

A really excellent technical book giving "Basic Information on Wood as a Material of Construction with Data for its Use in Design and Specification." 325 pages, last priced at 75¢, of tables, definitions, descriptions and illustrations and very comprehensive bibliographies.

Jones, Mack M. SHOPWORK ON THE FARM. New York: McGraw-Hill Book Company, Inc., 1945

Chapter 8 is an excellent introduction to concrete work; Chapter 3 is one of the best introductions to basic carpentry tools and how to use them. Clearly illustrated.

National Lumber Manufacturers Association. MANUAL FOR HOUSE FRAMING. Wood Construction Data No. 1. Washington: National Forest Products Association, Technical Services Division, 1961

Many illustrations of framing details, from floors to roofs, including staircases.

National Forest Products Association. PLANK-AND-BEAM FRAMING FOR RESIDENTIAL BUILDINGS. Washington: National Forest Products Association, Technical Services Division, 1970

Illustrated details of another system of framing, not so common as standard framing, but with advantages in cost and laborsaving..

Perth, L. THE STEEL SQUARE. New Britain, Connecticut: Stanley Tools, 1949

This little booklet, subtitled "How to Use the Stanley Rafter Square," is the best introduction to the use of the framing square. Lots of definitions and illustrations, 46 pages.

ARCHITECTURAL GRAPHIC STANDARDS (see bibliography at end of chapter 1.)

Sutcliffe, G. Lister, ed. THE MODERN CARPENTER JOINER AND CABINET-MAKER: A COMPLETE GUIDE TO CURRENT PRACTICE. London: The Gresham Publishing Co., 1900

Despite the fact that this large, 8 volume set was published so long ago, it remains the most comprehensive and encyclopedic work on the subject.

CARPENTERS AND BUILDERS LIBRARY (see bibliography at end of chapter 1.)

* May be ordered from the U.S. Government Printing Office.

The Roof Tree

In England, when the "last brick is laid," everybody concerned with the building of the house assembles, from architect to laborer, and a "topping out" party is held—at the owner's expense, with lots of back-slapping and drinking going on.

In Germany, and in fact, in many other countries, similar ceremonies take place when the highest part of the building is complete, and it is from Germany that the American custom of nailing a branch of evergreen to the first pair of rafters to be erected derives. This piece of evergreen is known as the roof tree, and while in olden days it was considered absolutely necessary to propitiate the gods for approaching too closely, it is now considered just good luck. Believe what you will, but do it—it looks nice.

CHAPTER THREE. *Sheathing*

When the framework of the house has been built it is ready for the SHEATH-ING. The sheathing is the outside covering, nailed directly to the studs and to the rafters, to which the final siding and the roofing materials are later applied.

There are operations which might be performed at this point, such as installing doors and windows, and building staircases, but for the sake of clarity these are all described in Chapter 7.

There are several types of sheathing, and indeed, some houses which have no sheathing at all, but the most common, and under most conditions the best, is plywood. Early American wooden houses, and most barns, often simply had the siding nailed directly to the framework and dispensed with sheathing.

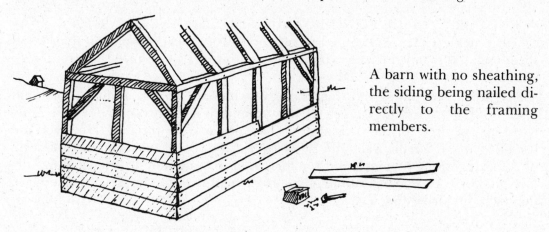

A barn with no sheathing, the siding being nailed directly to the framing members.

The next stage was the use of wooden boards, up to one inch thick and from six to ten inches wide, as sheathing; applied either horizontally, or for greater strength, diagonally.

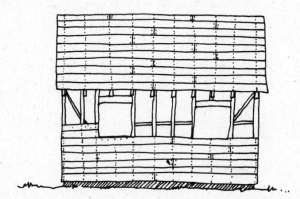

This sheathing should be started from the sill up, and fitted tightly together. Boards should be joined *over* framing members.

Nail boards on with 10d. common nails.

A house sheathed with horizontal boards.

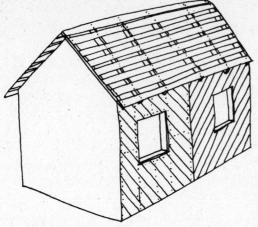

The sheathing on this roof, known as the ROOF BOARDS, is spaced and not tight as on the previous illustration. This may be done if wood shingles are to be used.

Note that the sheathing starts from *both* sides—this is the strongest way. Once again all joints must be made over framing members such as headers or studs.

A house sheathed diagonally.

STRUCTURAL INSULATING BOARD, or SHEATHING BOARD as it is also called, is made in 4′ x 8′ sheets, like plywood. It is quicker to put up than wood sheathing and is much cheaper than plywood but does not have the strength of either.

There are many grades and thicknesses of plywood. For sheathing, a plywood made with exterior glue is used. If the framing is 16″ on center, ⅜″ thick plywood may be used for the walls and ½″ thick plywood for the roof. However, the use of ½″ or ⅝″ for the walls and ⅝″ or ¾″ for the roof is most common because of the extra strength gained and the increased insulation and better nailing surface provided. Plywood sheathing gives great rigidity to the house and eliminates the need for corner bracing.

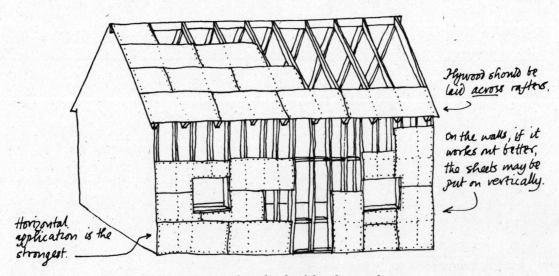

Plywood should be laid *across* rafters.

On the walls, if it works out better, the sheets may be put on vertically.

Horizontal application is the strongest.

A house sheathed with plywood.

On roofs plywood should be laid crossways to the rafters, as on floor joists, to tie the greatest number of framing members together with one sheet. On the walls, however, it may be installed vertically if this should be more economical and involve less work.

For ½″ to ¾″ thicknesses plywood should be nailed with 8d. common nails, 6″ on center around the edges of each sheet and 12″ on center to the intervening studs or rafters. All joints should be staggered as shown and centered on framing members. Although door and window openings will influence the positioning of the sheets, it is usually best to start from one corner and work along the wall. By nailing the bottom edge of the lowest sheets to the sill, the framework is securely tied to the foundation—since the sill is bolted to the top course of masonry.

If the framing has been erected perfectly plumb and level, then by lining up the edge of the first sheet of plywood with the outside corner it should be possible to place the subsequent sheets tightly against one another, all edges centering on studs. However, discrepancies sometimes arise and the thing to do is to average out the mistake, keeping the joints over the framework, nailing extra 2″ x 4″ 's to the studs to provide nailing surface if necessary.

The plywood should come flush to the inside edge of the rough openings (for doors and windows).

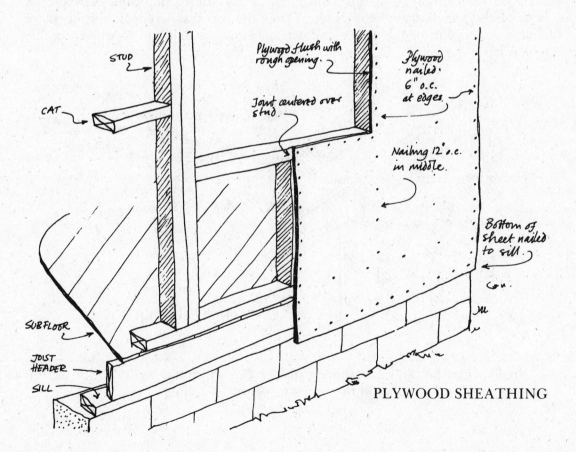

STUD

Plywood flush with rough opening.

Plywood nailed 6″ o.c. at edges.

CAT

Joint centered over stud.

Nailing 12″ o.c. in middle.

Bottom of sheet nailed to sill.

SUBFLOOR

JOIST HEADER

SILL

PLYWOOD SHEATHING

Sometimes it is more expedient to nail up whole sheets of plywood, disregarding the rough openings, cutting them out later. This often saves time but may result in considerable waste.

To make life easier—but more expensive—it is possible to obtain plywood with jointed edges. This provides greater strength along unsupported edges, but with framing 16″ on center and plywood ½″ thick or more, this is not absolutely necessary.

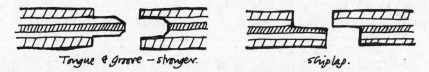

Tongue & groove — stronger.   shiplap.

TWO TYPES OF JOINTED EDGES
OF PLYWOOD PANELS

The important thing is that the sheathing be as continuous, flat, and tight together as is possible—by using large sections rather than piecing together lots of small bits. Usually, the only difficult part is at the top of the walls, between the ends of the rafters where they extend over the top plate. It may help to place nailers either side of the rafters as shown below, so that the plywood may be nailed more securely.

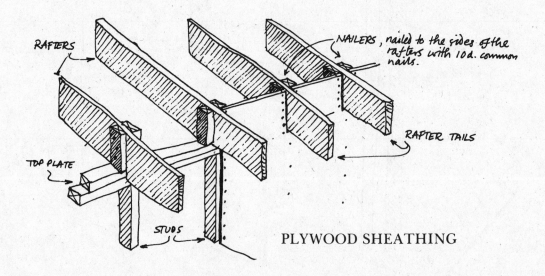

RAFTERS

NAILERS, nailed to the sides of the rafters with 10d. common nails.

RAFTER TAILS

TOP PLATE

STUDS

PLYWOOD SHEATHING

The nailers may be made from pieces of 2″ x 4″, and should be flush with the top edge of the rafter—as should the top edge of the sheathing.

When sheathing the roof, start at the eaves and work toward the ridge. Lay the bottom sheet so that it projects ⅝″ past the end of the rafter. This will make the CORNICE work easier and better, later on.

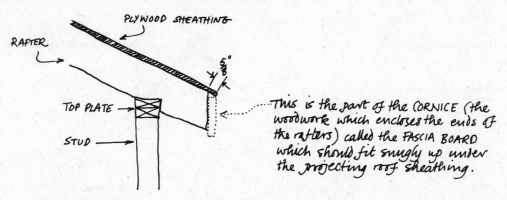

PLYWOOD SHEATHING

RAFTER

⅝″

TOP PLATE

STUD

This is the part of the CORNICE (the woodwork which encloses the ends of the rafters) called the FASCIA BOARD which should fit snugly up under the projecting roof sheathing.

At the gable ends (called the RAKE of the roof) the sheathing may extend past the end rafters, but should be supported by pieces of wood called TAILS, toe-nailed to the sides of the end rafters, no more than 4′ apart. Since fascia boards may be nailed to these tails, the sheathing must extend ¾″ over them.

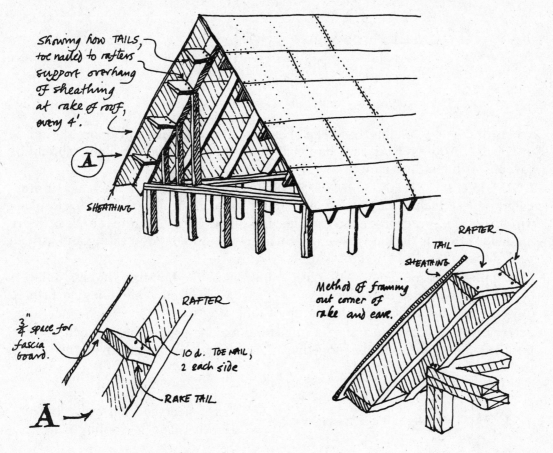

Showing how TAILS, toe nailed to rafters support overhang of sheathing at rake of roof, every 4′.

SHEATHING

Ⓐ

¾″ space for fascia board.

RAFTER

10 d. TOE NAIL, 2 each side

RAKE TAIL

A →

Method of framing out corner of rake and eave.

RAFTER

TAIL

SHEATHING

Make the joint at the ridge of the roof as close as is practical, but do not worry if it is not perfectly tight.

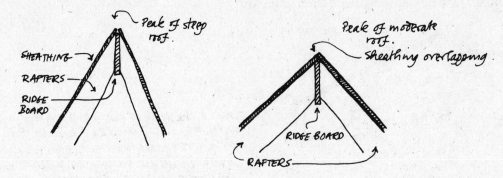

The most important thing in sheathing the roof is that the outside edges, at the rakes and the eaves, be as straight as possible, projecting evenly all around. This will make the shingling and the cornice work much easier.

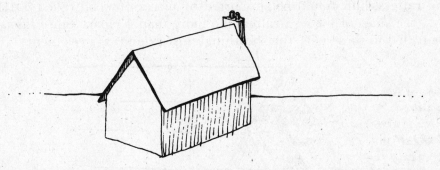

When the whole building has been sheathed, the windows and doors should be installed—this is explained in chapter 7—and then the whole building should be covered with building paper.

BUILDING PAPER (also known as TAR PAPER or FELT) is a black, tar impregnated paper which is water resistant, but not vapor resistant, which helps insulate, windproof and waterproof the building but allows it to "breathe". Rolls of it are made in different thicknesses, or weights; for use under wood siding and asphalt roof shingles the 15 lb. weight is used.

It is applied horizontally, starting at the bottom of the building, successive layers being lapped 4″ or so over the previous layers. Very often, white lines are printed on the paper to facilitate the lining up of long lengths.

Alternatively, a heavy duty stapling machine may be used. This is much quicker, but the staples must be closer together than the nails or the paper will tear off in the wind.

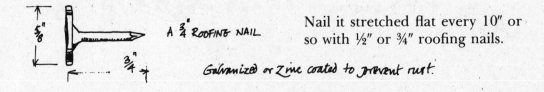

Nail it stretched flat every 10″ or so with ½″ or ¾″ roofing nails.

It is a good idea to try and paper on a mild day. If the weather is too cold the paper becomes brittle and tears easily; if the weather is too hot the paper becomes soft—and tears easily!

If there is to be a long wait before the siding or shingles are applied, and it is at all windy in your area, it will be better to use the roofing nails with ROOFING TINS. These are thin metal discs through which the nails are hammered to help prevent the paper from tearing off the building.

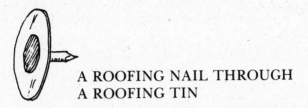

A ROOFING NAIL THROUGH
A ROOFING TIN

The roof is papered * the same way as the walls, taking care to overlap all layers from top to bottom, and the ridge at both sides, so that water runs over the paper and not under.

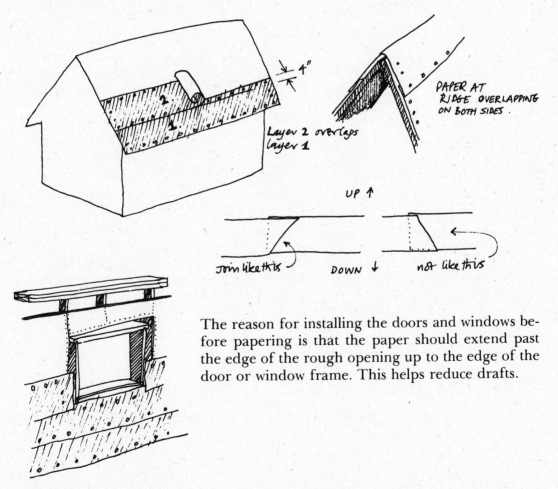

The reason for installing the doors and windows before papering is that the paper should extend past the edge of the rough opening up to the edge of the door or window frame. This helps reduce drafts.

* If cedar shingles are going on the roof, use ROSIN PAPER instead of tar paper. Rosin paper permits the shingles to breathe and thus last longer.

BIBLIOGRAPHY

American Plywood Association, PLYWOOD SHEATHING FOR FLOORS, WALLS AND ROOFS. Tacoma, Washington: American Plywood Association, 1967
This is only one of the many booklets available from the American Plywood Association covering most aspects of plywood application. Informative and authoritative.

ARCHITECTURAL GRAPHIC STANDARDS (see bibliography at end of chapter 1.)

CARPENTERS AND BUILDERS LIBRARY (see bibliography at end of chapter 1). Volume IV is especially useful concerning the techniques of wooden sheathing.

CHAPTER FOUR. *Siding*

The siding is the exterior covering of the walls of a house. It is most usually made of wood, although aluminum siding is becoming increasingly popular because of its long-lasting finish, and more expensive houses sometimes use a veneer of masonry—brick, stone or stucco.

Traditional wood siding may consist of the following types:

1. Plain, square-edged boards nailed horizontally, called CLAPBOARD SIDING.

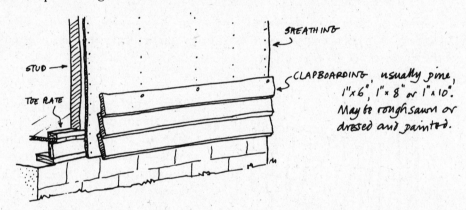

SHEATHING

STUD

TOE PLATE

CLAPBOARDING, usually pine, 1"x6", 1"x8" or 1"x10". May be rough sawn or dressed and painted.

2. Square-edged boards nailed vertically, narrower strips called BATTENS covering the joints between the wider boards. This form of siding is known as BOARD AND BATTEN.

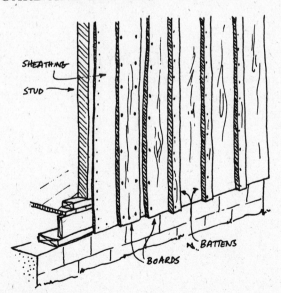

SHEATHING

STUD

BATTENS

BOARDS

BOARD AND BATTEN, pine or hemlock, cedar or redwood. The boards may be random widths, up to 12″ wide, and the battens are usually 1″ x 2″ or 1″ x 3″.

This kind of siding is usually left raw, or stained and treated with creosote—a wood preservative.

3. BEVEL SIDING is most often made from cedar, which weathers extremely well, and so is often left unpainted like clapboarding and board and batten.

BEVEL SIDING

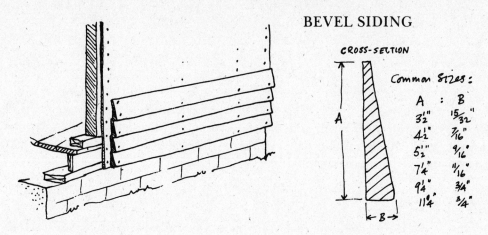

4. CEDAR SHINGLES are also used as siding, particularly in coastal areas because of their resistance to rot. They also come in many grades and sizes.*

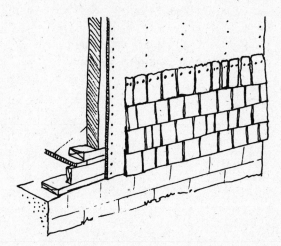

(The building paper applied over the sheathing—omitted for the sake of clarity in these illustrations—must not be used with shingles. Instead, ROSIN PAPER must be used—as on shingle roofs.)

5. PLYWOOD PANELLING has become very popular with many builders because of the speed with which large areas may be covered. It is made in many patterns and often requires no treatment such as painting. However, it is expensive to buy although it may save on labor costs.

* See Bibliography.

6. Probably the commonest form of wood siding is DROP SIDING. This consists of horizontal boards, usually painted, shiplapped to fit tightly the one over the other, and made in a variety of sizes and patterns—all basically similar, such as RUSTIC, DROP and NOVELTY SIDING.

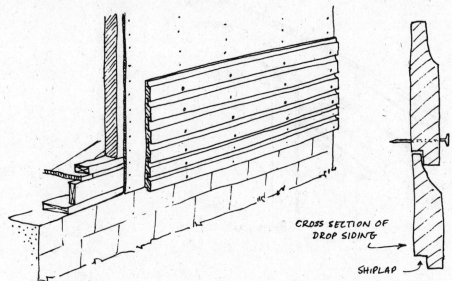

CROSS SECTION OF
DROP SIDING

SHIPLAP

Most drop siding is made from western pine.

Before any siding can be erected there will be a certain amount of TRIM WORK to be done—how much depending on what kind of siding is used and your own taste. Trim work is the name given to the woodwork around the outside edges of doors and windows, the corners of the house, sometimes the bottom of the siding, and the CORNICE—the woodwork which covers the rafter ends at the eaves and the rakes.

1. The Cornice.

If the rafter ends are to be boxed in, the cornice is the first trim work to be done, since the corner boards and the siding butt up against it, and it is difficult to make a snug fit against something which is not there yet.

Cornices were originally imitative of the stone cornices of European buildings, built to support heavy roofs, and consequently were often very elaborate, consisting of many fancy moldings.

Basically, a cornice consists of the following parts: FASCIA, SOFFIT, FRIEZE, SHINGLE and BED MOLDINGS.

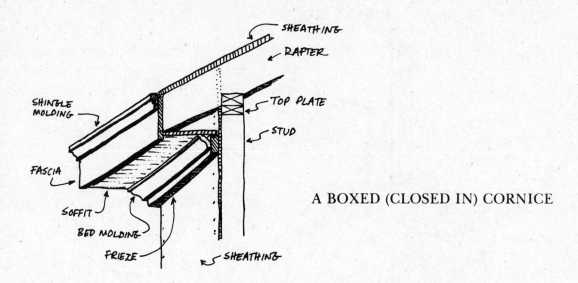

A BOXED (CLOSED IN) CORNICE

The cornice construction details will depend on the length and cut of the rafter tail. A close look at some old elegant wooden buildings will show the extreme variation in cornices.

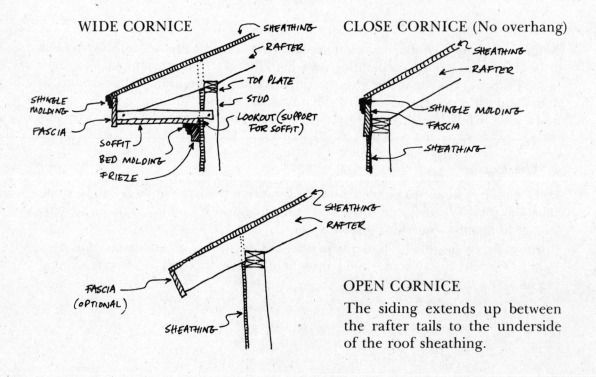

OPEN CORNICE

The siding extends up between the rafter tails to the underside of the roof sheathing.

If you do build a cornice, the fascia is the first part to make. This must be at least as wide as the rafters, and is usually made from 1″ thick, dressed lumber. If the building is too long for one piece to reach from end to end, the pieces must be butted together over rafter ends. The fascia should fit snugly up under the projecting edge of the roof sheathing, and if the pitch is steep the top edge should be beveled for a close fit—unless the rafter end is cut square.

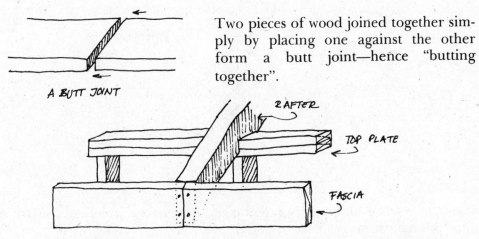

A BUTT JOINT

Two pieces of wood joined together simply by placing one against the other form a butt joint—hence "butting together".

2 AFTER

TOP PLATE

FASCIA

TWO PIECES OF FASCIA BOARD BUTTED TIGHTLY TOGETHER AT A RAFTER END
(Roof and wall sheathing removed.)

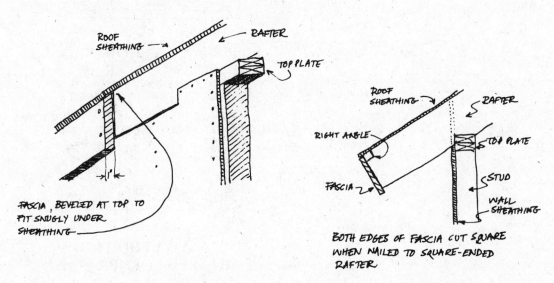

ROOF SHEATHING

RAFTER

TOP PLATE

FASCIA, BEVELED AT TOP TO FIT SNUGLY UNDER SHEATHING

ROOF SHEATHING

RAFTER

RIGHT ANGLE

TOP PLATE

FASCIA

STUD

WALL SHEATHING

BOTH EDGES OF FASCIA CUT SQUARE WHEN NAILED TO SQUARE-ENDED RAFTER

To nail the fascia use two 10d. *galvanized* common nails at each rafter end. This is to prevent the nail from rusting and staining the wood or paint.

What happens to the cornice at the gable ends of the roof depends on how much rake (overhang) there is. The easiest way with an overhanging rake is to continue the cornice up the gable, using the tails which support the rake in the same way as the rafter ends at the eaves.

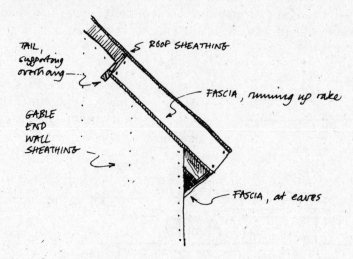

If the cornice is to be continued up the rake, the corners of the fascia boards may be simply butted or, more nicely, mitered.

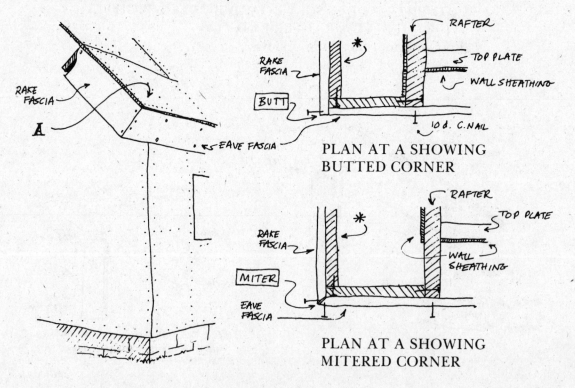

PLAN AT A SHOWING
BUTTED CORNER

PLAN AT A SHOWING
MITERED CORNER

* See previous chapter for framing out corner of rake and eave.

A close look at old buildings will show a wide variety of trim detail at the rake projection for cornices. Many employ some kind of CORNICE RETURN, as shown below.

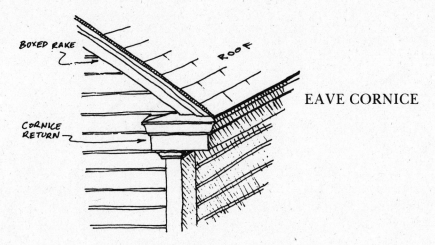

If the fascia is made so that it projects below the bottom of the rafter, the soffit will be able to be fitted up against it tightly.

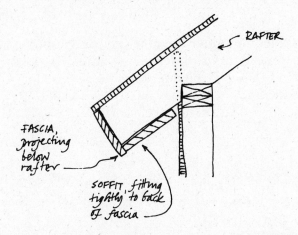

Nail the soffit the same way as the fascia, using two 10d. galvanized common nails to every rafter, and butting the joints over rafters. Although the soffit should fit snugly to the fascia, the edge nearest the building is not so critical since it can be covered by the FRIEZE BOARD, usually made from lumber thicker than the siding—in order to form a wider seat for the siding.

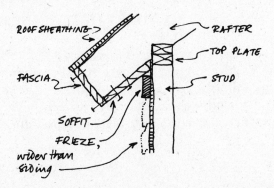

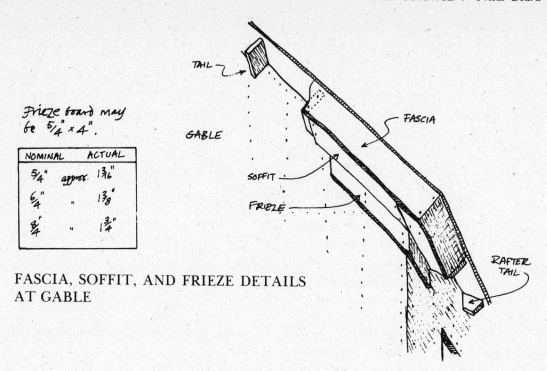

Frieze board may
be 5/4" × 4".

NOMINAL	ACTUAL
5/4"	approx. 1 3/16"
6/4"	" 1 3/8"
8/4"	" 1 3/4"

FASCIA, SOFFIT, AND FRIEZE DETAILS AT GABLE

If the frieze is continued up under the rake the corner should be mitered like the fascia. Nail the frieze to the studs under the sheathing for greatest strength. Once again, for the nicest work, bevel the top of the frieze board to fit snugly under the soffit. This is unnecessary, of course, if the soffit is nailed horizontally to a lookout support.

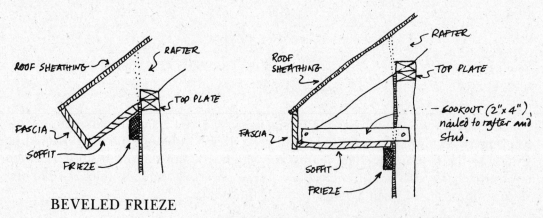

BEVELED FRIEZE

SQUARE FRIEZE UNDER HORIZONTAL SOFFIT

After the fascia, soffit, and frieze are in place the shingle and bed moldings may be applied. Shingle molding is nailed to the top of the fascia and covers the joint between it and the roof sheathing. Functionally, it need be little more than a plain piece of 1" x 2"; in practice, it is very often a shaped molding, bought from a lumberyard or made up specially by hand, using a molding plane—of which there are many types, each producing a different shape—or by a machine, such as a router or a shaper—two power tools designed specifically to cut moldings.

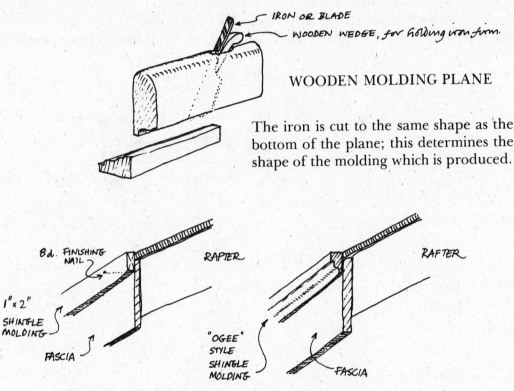

IRON OR BLADE
WOODEN WEDGE, for holding iron firm.

WOODEN MOLDING PLANE

The iron is cut to the same shape as the bottom of the plane; this determines the shape of the molding which is produced.

8d. FINISHING NAIL

RAFTER

RAFTER

1" x 2" SHINGLE MOLDING

"OGEE" STYLE SHINGLE MOLDING

FASCIA

FASCIA

TWO WAYS OF MAKING SHINGLE MOLDING

Bed Molding is the molding which is sometimes added at the meeting of the soffit and the frieze, and like the shingle molding, may be plain or fancy. A common type used by many builders, and in stock at most lumberyards, is CROWN MOLDING.

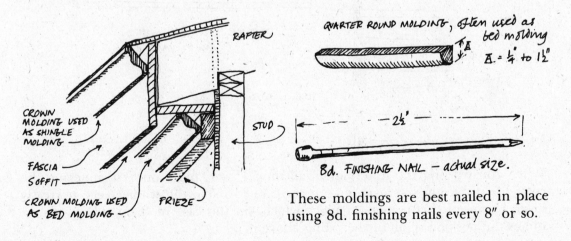

RAFTER

CROWN MOLDING USED AS SHINGLE MOLDING

FASCIA

SOFFIT

CROWN MOLDING USED AS BED MOLDING

FRIEZE

STUD

QUARTER ROUND MOLDING, often used as bed molding
A = $\frac{1}{4}$ to $1\frac{1}{2}$"

— $2\frac{1}{2}$" —

8d. FINISHING NAIL — actual size.

These moldings are best nailed in place using 8d. finishing nails every 8" or so.

If the rafter ends are to be enclosed in a cornice, provision must be made now for ventilation. Ventilation is explained in chapter 6 more fully. All that needs to be done now is to drill holes between each pair of rafters—2 holes, 1″ in diameter, are sufficient if the rafters are 16″ on center—and insert a louver in the soffit (between each pair of rafters). This provides free access for air into the roof. The louver (sometimes pieces of screening are used) prevents insects from entering.

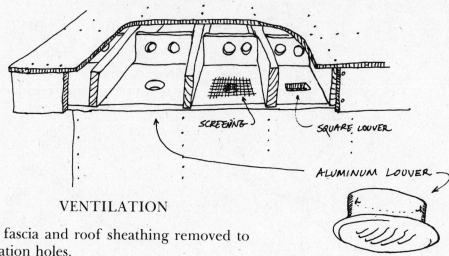

VENTILATION

Part of the fascia and roof sheathing removed to show ventilation holes.

2. The Watertable.

Well-constructed buildings have watertables around the base of the siding. A watertable is not absolutely essential but is good practice since it adds to the appearance of the house and helps prevent the bottom of the siding from rotting out by providing a drip edge.

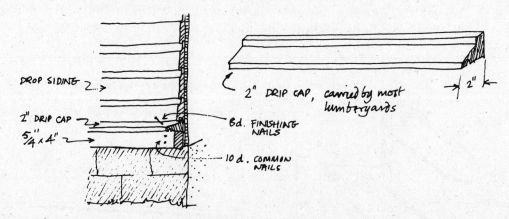

When constructing the watertable, nail the ⁵/₄″ x 4″ piece on first, mitering the corners, and using the level, take great care to make the whole piece perfectly level, because it is this bottom piece which—in the case of drop siding—determines the position of all of the siding above it.

3. The Corner Boards.

The corners of the building should be trimmed out with corner boards, sometimes made from 1″ x 4″, but in better buildings made from ⁵/₄″ x 4″. These boards extend from the watertable (or the bottom of the siding, if there is no watertable) to the frieze board (or underneath of the roof sheathing, if there is no cornice.) There are three methods, shown below.

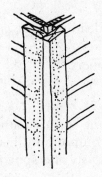

1. Nail the Corner Boards, butted, the one to the other as shown, OVER the siding.

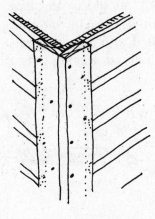

2. Nail the corner boards to the house, THEN butt the siding up to the corner boards.

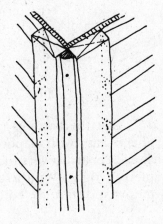

3. The most elegant of all three ways is to nail each board so that its outside edge is flush with the corner of the house, and then nail, with 8d. finishing nails, a piece of ¼″ round molding in the very corner.

All three methods may be used for inside corners. Care should be taken, and the spirit level used, to ensure that the corner boards are nailed up *perfectly* plumb.

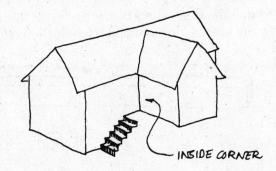

INSIDE CORNER

4. The Window and Door Trim.

Window and door trim should be made and fitted before the siding is nailed up. This is dealt with fully in chapter 7.

SIDING APPLICATION

Siding, apart from board and batten siding, and plywood siding, is always started from the bottom up.

It should be nailed into the studs or other framing members.

Short lengths should always end over studs.

Two vertical joints should never align.

If it is to be painted, the nails should be punched below the surface with a nail set and the holes filled with a good grade of putty or wood compound. Cheap grades tend to dry and fall out, leaving the nail head to become rusty and spoil the looks.

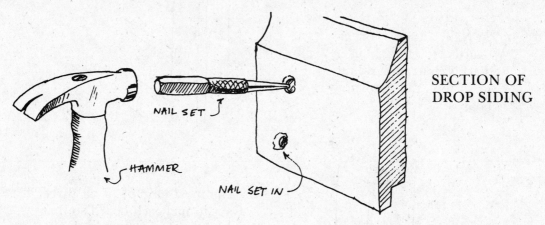

SECTION OF
DROP SIDING

NAIL SET

HAMMER

NAIL SET IN

Horizontal types of siding should be spaced so that the bottoms of boards run level with the tops of windows and doors. This is easy with clapboarding, bevel siding and shingles since the amount by which each board covers the one below— the lap—may be adjusted to make it all come out right. With drop siding you should measure down from the top of the window and start the bottom board accordingly.

If the sheathing has been put up carefully and level at its bottom edge it will be easy to nail the first siding board on level. In any event it is always a good idea to ensure the siding's horizontalness with the level.

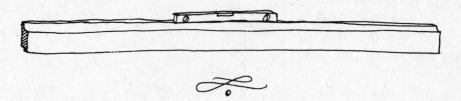

BIBLIOGRAPHY

HOME PAINTING, WALL PAPERING AND DECORATING. New York: Wm. H. Wise & Co., 1951

This book has some excellent illustrations of ladders, scaffolding, and other means of reaching all parts of the outside of buildings. There is also useful information on exterior siding painting and finishing.

ARCHITECTURAL GRAPHIC STANDARDS (see bibliography at end of chapter 1.)

CARPENTERS AND BUILDERS LIBRARY (see bibliography at end of chapter 1.)

CERTI-SPLIT MANUAL OF HANDSPLIT RED CEDAR SHAKES (see bibliography at end of chapter 5.)

In *very* olden days there existed a custom, similar to that of the roof tree, of making sure that the gods were propitiated properly when houses were begun, by burying a virgin in the foundation. The custom has died out, (!) though records remain attesting the fact, and yet the vestiges of our ancestors' concern may be seen in the habit of burying a few coin of the realm under the first block laid, when the foundation is begun.

The Foundation Offering

CHAPTER FIVE. *Roofing*

Roofs may be surfaced with a variety of materials including metal, slate, clay, wood, tar or straw. The most common roofing material used for small houses is asphalt-felt shingles coated with a layer of mineral granules. This is preferred because of its relative cheapness, quickness of application, and low fire risk. Before describing the application of asphalt shingles, however, mention will be made of some of the other materials. For information concerning the application of these refer to the bibliography.

1. Metal.

Different metals used for roofing include galvanized iron, tin, aluminum, copper, zinc and Monel. While metal roofs are watertight and long-lasting, they are expensive and often annoyingly noisy during rainstorms.

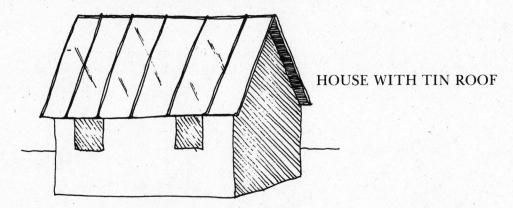

HOUSE WITH TIN ROOF

2. Slate and Tile.

Slate and tile are often used for large, permanent buildings. Slate is more commonly used on stone or brick buildings as it is very heavy but exceedingly long-lasting. Tile, made from burnt clay, and sometimes concrete, is common in the south and west.

MISSION TILED HOUSE

3. Wood.

Wood, riven into shakes and shingles, was one of the earliest roofing materials used in America, and is long-lasting and beautiful but can constitute a fire hazard and also has become very expensive.

SHINGLE:
sawn both sides.

SHAKE:
handsplit one side,
sawn the other.

WOOD SHINGLES:
made from Red
Cedar or Redwood.

4. Straw.

Thatched roofs have been made for hundreds of years and provide a waterproof and well-insulated roof; but they are a BIG fire hazard and tend to harbor insects. Moreover, it is a difficult technique and there are few qualified thatchers left.

THATCHED COTTAGE

5. Tar.

Layers of tar impregnated felt and hot tar provide one of the best coverings for flat and low pitched roofs. This can be a messy business and for regular pitched roofs asphalt shingles are far cheaper and quicker to lay.

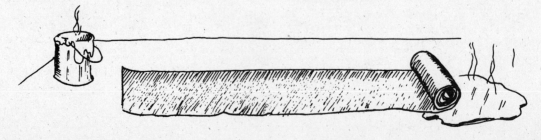

6. Asphalt Shingles.

PREPARATION

A number of things must be done before shingles may be applied to a roof. Firstly, the sheathing should be firm and smooth, with no gaps between boards or sheets of plywood, and no nails projecting.

Secondly, for a good job, 15 lb. building paper should be laid, as described in chapter 3. For added quality the paper may be cemented to the edges of the sheathing with asphalt cement—available in 5 gallon cans, and which you will need if there is any flashing to be done.

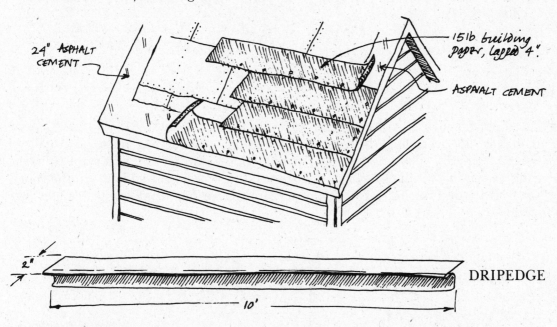

Thirdly, DRIPEDGE is made of galvanized steel or aluminum—which can be obtained painted white. It is made in 10′ lengths and slightly different widths—the wider the better (although 4″ is the recommended width, the most commonly available width is 2″). Its purpose is to support the edges of the shingles, secure the building paper to the roof and most important—as its name implies—to allow the water to drip off the roof rather than run down the side of the cornice and discolor or damage the woodwork.

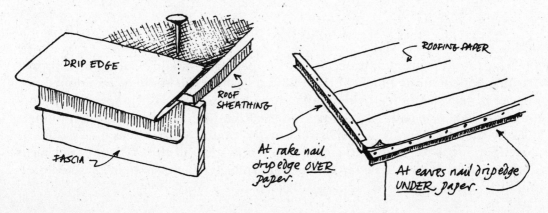

To avoid corrosion of the metal through galvanic action, if aluminum dripedge is used, the nails should be aluminum; and if galvanized steel is used then galvanized roofing nails should be applied. In either case nail the dripedge tight to the edge of the roof, using a nail just long enough to go through the paper and the sheathing, about one every 10″. The dripedge is cut easily with tin snips, metal shears or even a hacksaw. When two lengths are joined at the rake, lap the higher piece *over* the lower, so the water runs off and not under.

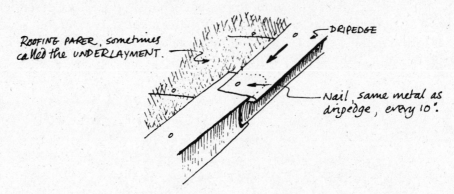

Fourthly, in preparing the roof for shingling, FLASHING must be installed where necessary. Flashing is usually metal (copper, aluminum, and rarely, tin) in rolls of varying width (10″, 12″, 14″ etc.,) used to waterproof all joints in the roof, such as the intersection of different roof lines, dormer windows, vent pipes, or chimneys.

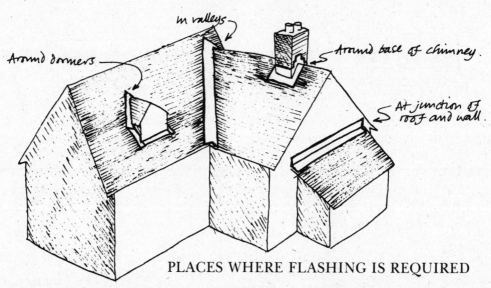

PLACES WHERE FLASHING IS REQUIRED

Once again, to prevent galvanic action, copper nails should be used with copper flashing and aluminum nails with aluminum flashing. It should be mentioned that copper is many times the price of aluminum, and while it lasts longer than aluminum the cost is usually prohibitive for small houses. In fact while aluminum is sold by the foot length, copper is sold by the pound weight. Flashing should be cut, when it has to go around corners, so that water will run *over* the lower piece and not *under*. It should be set in a bed of asphalt cement (sometimes called roofing tar) with all joints overlapping at least 6″.

When all of the above has been attended to the shingling may start.

Asphalt shingles are made in strips or singles and include the following patterns:

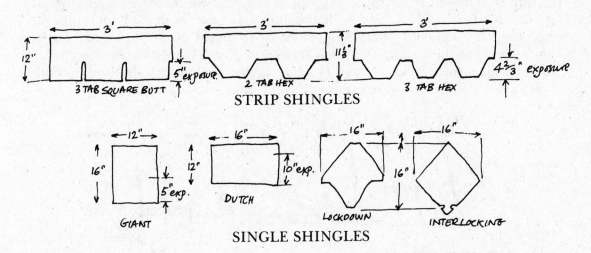

STRIP SHINGLES

SINGLE SHINGLES

Three tab square butt strip shingles are the commonest and easiest to apply. They are sold by the SQUARE. A square of shingles being the amount needed to cover 100 square feet of roof. They are wrapped in packets, 3 to a square. For example, the roof below measures 10' x 20'. The total square area is therefore 10 x 20 x 2 (because there are 2 sides) which equals 400 sq. ft., or 4 squares, or 12 packets which may be stacked as shown, but never more than 4' high, or they might squash in the heat.

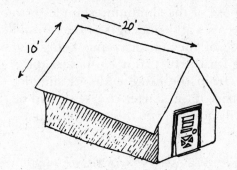

Since wind is any roof covering's worst enemy, the better grades of shingles are provided with a dab of tar underneath each tab which eventually adheres to the shingle below.

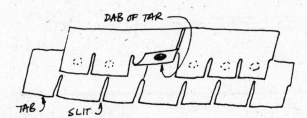

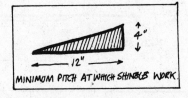

There are a wide range of colors available, including black and white. If you plan to have an uninsulated attic remember that white reflects the heat and black tends to absorb it, and would make the attic *very* warm.

APPLICATION

1. Buy a bundle of cedar shimming shingles. These are wooden shingles which are not good enough for the roof (or wall) and are sold in single bundles for all the numerous occasions when things must be shimmed up or out a little. Lay a course (row) of these shingles so that they overhang ½″ at the eaves and are ¼″ apart (to allow for swelling when they get wet). Nail them with galvanized roofing nails, 2 to a shingle, and take care to keep the edge which projects straight.

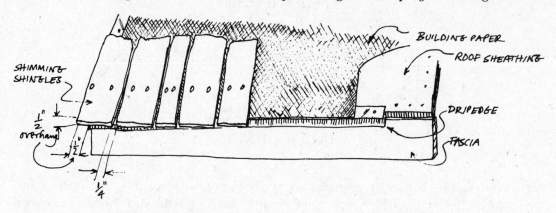

2. After a course of shimming shingles has been laid the starter course of asphalt shingles is laid. This consists of a row of shingles laid flush with the edge of the shimming shingles, but upside down. The purpose of the shimming shingles is so that the asphalt shingles may project over the eaves and not sag—as they would eventually do if left unsupported. The purpose of the starter course being laid upside down is to provide a continuous backing for the first course uninterrupted by the slits. It is easiest to start every course from the same end. All shingles should overhang the rake about ½″. The first strip of the starter course should be ½ strip, so that the joints of the first course will not lie over the starter course's joints.

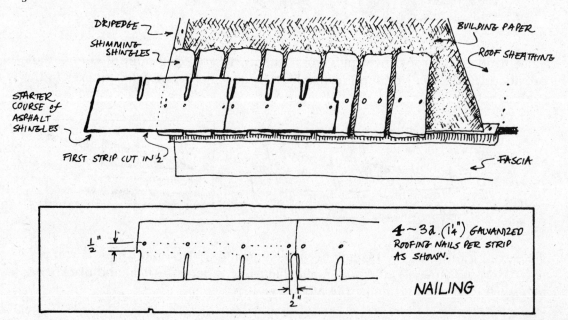

3. The next layer is the first course proper. This is laid, right way up, over the starter course, starting with a whole strip. Butt each strip tightly up against the preceding strip so that all the slits will appear equal. Some strips have half a slit at both ends and others have a full slit at one end and a square cut at the other; when all the shingles are laid it should be impossible to tell where the joints are by looking at the slits.

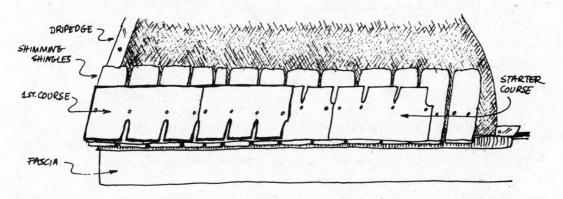

4. The second course of shingles begins with a strip from which ⅓ of the first tab is cut off. This is done so that the joints of subsequent courses never lie directly over one another. The amount of the first course left uncovered should be 5″. This is called "an exposure of 5″ to the weather."

5. The third course completes the cycle, for the fourth course duplicates the first, the fifth the second, and so on. The first strip of the third course has ⅔ of the first tab cut off. (The fourth course starts—like the first—with an entire strip.)

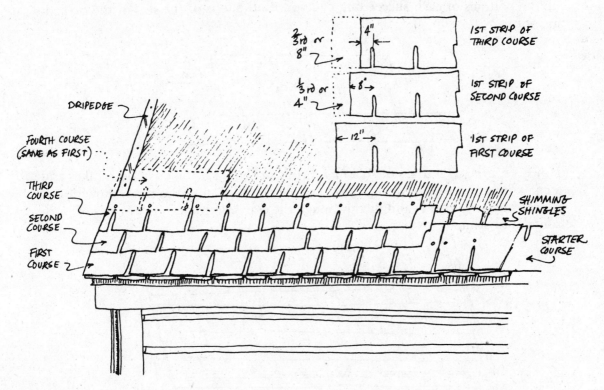

As with tar paper, in hot weather the shingles will tear easily and in cold weather they will become very brittle and crack apart if not handled carefully. The easiest way to cut them is to turn them over and use a framing square and a mat knife as shown:

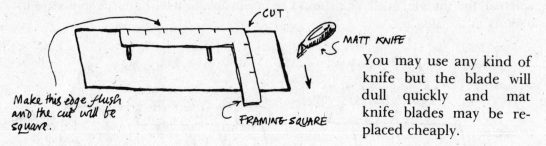

You may use any kind of knife but the blade will dull quickly and mat knife blades may be replaced cheaply.

By scoring the shingle deeply it may be folded and broken off cleanly. The reason for turning the shingle over is that if you cut through the mineral granules with which the front of the shingle is coated the knife would wear out much quicker.

To emphasize the main points to remember:

1. The starter course and the first course should be flush with the edge of the shimming shingles which should overhang the roof by about ½".

2. The shingles should overhang the rake by about ½".

3. The strips should be butted tightly to one another.

4. The amount of shingle left exposed to the weather depends on the pitch of the roof and the thickness of the shingle. This is usually tabulated on the packet. Thicker shingles are better than thinner ones since they last longer. In general the exposure should be 5"—which is the depth of a slit, which makes it easy to line up the bottoms of each succeeding course with the tops of the slits of the preceding course.

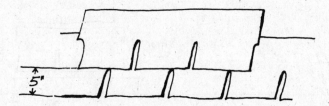

However, every 6 courses or so a measurement should be taken at both rakes and a chalk line snapped between them marking the bottom of the next course, for it is amazing how quickly and by how much the courses can get wavy or out of horizontal and slanted.

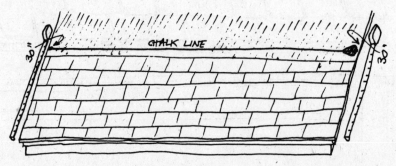

When both sides of the roof have been shingled as far as the ridge, the cap course must be made. Cut strips into 3 tabs and nail the tabs sideways, an equal amount on both sides, with the open end away from the prevailing weather.

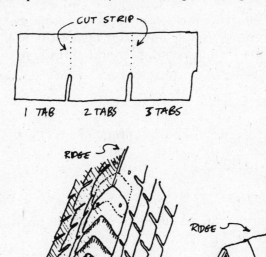

TWO VIEWS
OF THE CAP
COURSE

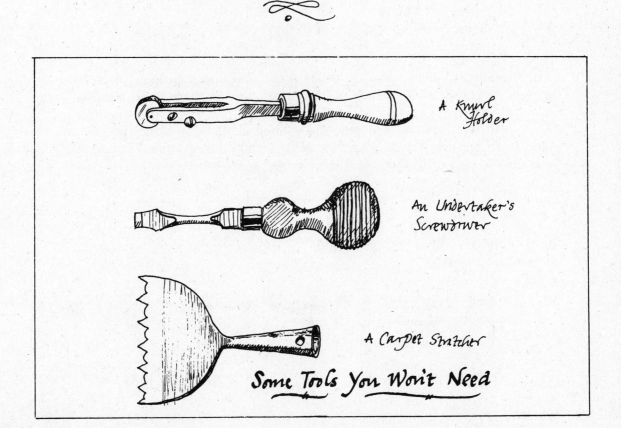

GUTTERS

Gutters collect the rain from a roof and lead it to storage—such as a cistern or a rain barrel—to a drain, or simply any place out of the way, thus preventing the area around the house from becoming too wet and soggy.

Wooden gutters are made from rot-resistant woods such as cedar, redwood or fir.

   SECTION OF WOODEN GUTTER

Older houses, and large modern buildings often have built-in gutters—built at the eaves *behind* the cornice.

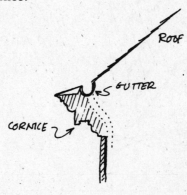

The easiest and cheapest way is to install galvanized gutters; these may be painted, secured to the fascia, or the rafter ends if there is no cornice. Large houses with great expanses of roof require that the gutters and the downspouts be of sufficient capacity to handle the volume of water and that the downspouts be of sufficient frequency to carry it away. Small houses, up to 30′ long, are adequately serviced with standard 5″ gutters and one downspout.

Gutters may be halfround or "K" pattern:

Downspouts may be round, rectangular,
plain or corrugated:

HALF ROUND   "K" pattern

PLAIN ROUND   CORRUGATED ROUND

SECTIONS OF DOWNSPOUTS   PLAIN RECTANGULAR   CORRUGATED RECTANGULAR

In cold climates where there is a possibility of standing water freezing in the downspouts the corrugated type is preferable since it will expand without damage.

The different parts of a roof drainage system are:

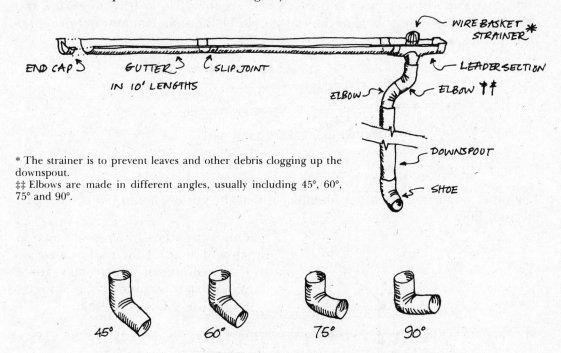

* The strainer is to prevent leaves and other debris clogging up the downspout.

‡‡ Elbows are made in different angles, usually including 45°, 60°, 75° and 90°.

Supports for the gutter are varied and adaptable to different situations. The most usual is a bracket or hanger which is screwed to the fascia and which holds the gutter with a spring clip.

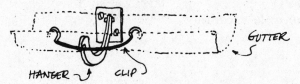

Downspouts are held in place by straps or large hooks nailed to the side of the house.

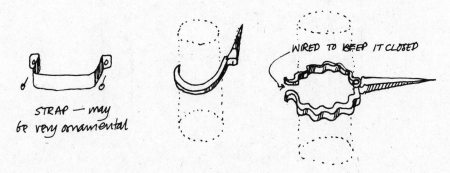

When hanging the gutters the lengths may be easily cut to length with a hacksaw or a pair of tinsnips. Start from the high end and slope the gutter a minimum of $^1/_{16}''$ for every foot of run. Be careful not to let any lengths slope upwards or pools of water will rest there and rust out the gutter. Use a level to ensure the slope is uniform—the bubble in the vial should be the same amount out of center at all points along the gutter.

The other important point to remember is that the gutter should not project past the roof line.

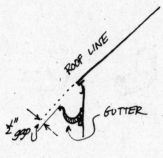

Otherwise the gutter will impede snow sliding off the roof and an ice dam will result which may force water back up under the shingles and cause the roof to leak.

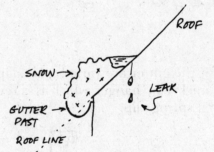

The steeper the pitch the less clearance is necessary.

12-12 pitch requires ¼″ clearance
12-7   "   ½″   "
12-5   "   ¾″   "

When fitting together the various sections of the downspout, fit the upper piece into the lower piece—so that water will run down *inside* the pipe.

BIBLIOGRAPHY

Clark, Donald H., CERTI-SPLIT MANUAL OF HANDSPLIT RED CEDAR SHAKES. Seattle, Washington: Red Cedar Shingle and Handsplit Shake Bureau, 1971
This manual, which may be obtained with much other free material, directly from one of the largest shingle manufacturers, is comprehensive and instructive.

ARCHITECTURAL GRAPHIC STANDARDS (see bibliography at end of chapter 1.)

CARPENTERS AND BUILDERS LIBRARY (see bibliography at end of chapter 1.)

Practically all big lumber companies give these useful aprons away free as advertising.

A CARPENTER'S APRON

Some Useful Equipment

Many lumber yards make sawhorses out of their scrap lumber cheaper than you could.

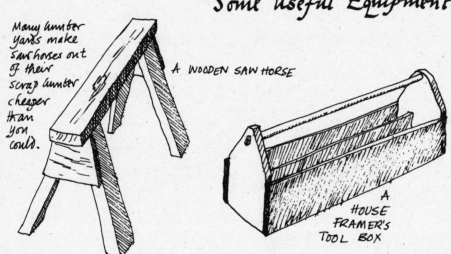

A WOODEN SAW HORSE

A HOUSE FRAMER'S TOOL BOX

Don't try to carry too many tools in these boxes, they get very heavy very quickly & it's hard to find things at the bottom

CHAPTER SIX. *The Works*

This chapter is about things which may be best left to professionals. However, anyone building a house should know at least enough to make the necessary provisions for these various services and in what order they should be done.

The subjects covered are: **ELECTRICAL WIRING, PLUMBING,** and **HEATING.** In addition, **INSULATION, VENTILATION,** and **BACKFILLING** are discussed since these operations must be coordinated with the wiring and plumbing, etc.

ELECTRICAL WIRING

Wiring is in many ways the most complicated and potentially dangerous part of housebuilding, and for these reasons should only be attempted by someone completely qualified.

The best advice that may be given is that proper planning will save time and money, so consult a qualified electrician—in many areas he will be required to be licensed—as soon as possible.

While you will not be able to have electricity in the house until much of it is built, it makes things much easier to have electricity at the site from the beginning. Power may be brought to the site underground or by poles, it being much cheaper to use poles. Pole installation should be arranged with a pole erection company in consultation with yourself and the local utility company. You may have preferences as to the location of the poles based on the view, the erection company will know which is the easiest route in the event of wooded areas or hilly terrain, and the utility company will have its own requirements. Circumstances vary greatly but in general poles are spaced about 150′ apart. They usually belong to you and are your responsibility, but sometimes other arrangements may be made with the utility company or your neighbors.

The last pole before the house should not be more than 125′ away. Its exact location will depend on the site and whether you plan to have underground service to the house or overhead wires.

Your electrician will install a "temporary service" on this last pole and from it you will be able to get electricity while you are building—to run cement mixers, power saws and lights, etc.

From this point the consideration is whether to bring the power to the house over, or underground. If overhead service is decided upon then the siding must be completed so that the "weatherhead" may be fixed to the house.

THE WEATHERHEAD,
FIXED TO THE
OUTSIDE OF THE HOUSE,
THROUGH WHICH THE POWER
LINES ENTER THE HOUSE.

THE WEATHERHEAD, FIXED TO THE OUTSIDE OF THE HOUSE, THROUGH WHICH THE POWER LINES ENTER THE HOUSE.

Every aspect of wiring is carefully governed by the National Electrical Code, and everything must be inspected by the Fire Underwriters Laboratory Inspectors before most utility companies will connect the power. Your electrician will advise you on any provisions which must be made to ensure adherence to the rules—for example, there are minimum heights at which overhead lines may be hung, and stipulations as to where the weatherhead may be affixed—generally to that part of the house closest to the last pole.

Similarly, if you decide to bring the power underground to the house—which is a little more expensive but longer-lasting, safer from weather and other damage,

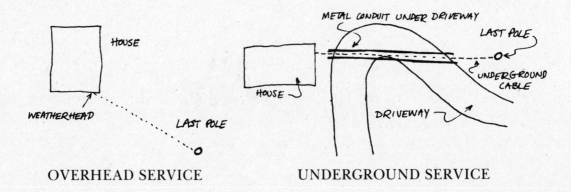

OVERHEAD SERVICE   **UNDERGROUND SERVICE**

and better looking,—there are other specific requirements to be met. For example, the cable must be at least 18″ below grade, and if it is to be under a driveway it must be protected in metal conduit.

This is something you should plan together with the excavator and the electrician in order to have all the excavating and covering over again (known as backfilling) done with the least amount of visits by the bulldozer—since this is expensive. The plumber should be consulted at this time too, so that provision may be made for digging trenches to the well or water supply, and installing any wiring needed for a pump.

Ideally, the excavator should dig not only the foundation, but all service trenches and drainage systems at the same time. When the foundations are built, the power lines, drains and septic tanks, etc., should be installed so that everything may be backfilled at the same time.

The first place the power goes in the house is to the distribution box, which is where all the various circuits begin, and where the fuses or circuit breakers,* including the main switch, are to be found. This is also called the loadcenter or panel box.

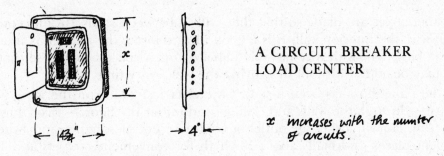

A CIRCUIT BREAKER
LOAD CENTER

x increases with the number of circuits.

Once again, there are specific requirements regulating its size, type and location. Your electrician will advise you, but you should plan all your needs in advance to determine what size box you will use. For example, a small house might be adequately served by a 100 amp service with 24 circuits, while a larger house, or a house with more electrical appliances, may need a 200 amp service with 42 circuits.

On the next page is a list containing many of the appliances you may want, now or in the future, and a careful consideration of these will enable your electrician to decide on the best size service for you.

---

* Almost all new installations now employ circuit breakers—which are switches that trip off when overloaded and need only to be switched back on again, instead of the old type of fuses which need to be either mended or replaced entirely.

Air conditioner	Juice extractor
Attic fan	Mixer
Clothes dryer	Oil burner
Dishwasher	Percolator
Disposer	Radio
Egg cooker	Range
Electric fan	Refrigerator
Freezer	Sunlamp
Furnace blower	Television
Grill	Toaster
Hair dryer	Vacuum cleaner
Heating pad	Waffle iron
Hot plate	Washing machine
Infra-red lamp	Water heater
Iron	Wringer

Some Possible Household Appliances

Most panel boxes are made so that they will fit between studs 16″ on center and be flush with the interior wall. It is a good idea to locate the panel box in a closet or in the basement with a removable panel or open space below it so that extra wiring may be added without destroying the wall every time.

When the panel box has been installed the electrician will run the wires around the house—through the walls and ceilings and under the floors—according to the wiring plan. He will install the outlet boxes for receptacles, lights, and switches at convenient places—normally about 14″ high for convenience outlets and 4′ high for switches. Outlets in the kitchen and bathroom and other special areas such as work rooms will vary and must be planned in accordance with your needs and the Code.

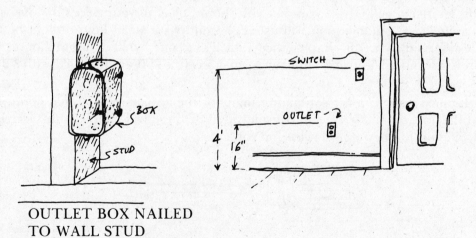

OUTLET BOX NAILED
TO WALL STUD

A few points to watch for are:

1. The wire should run through the *center* of the studs, and you must be careful not to nail through the wire later when applying inside, or outside, wall coverings.

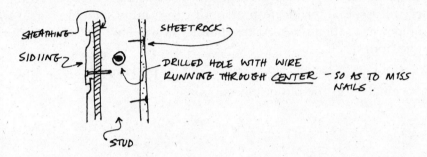

2. Wire running around bathtubs should be *below* the top of the tub to eliminate any chance of making contact with the wiring when subsequently putting long screws in the wall for soap dishes or towel racks, etc.

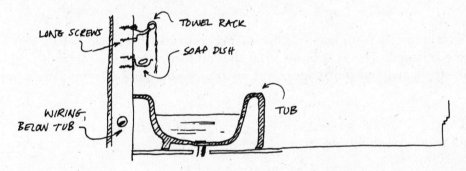

3. Wires should not run too close to the plumbing in order to avoid damage from the plumber's blow torch when he is working.

4. The electrician must know how you plan to finish the walls so that he may set the boxes to project the right amount through the finish wall.

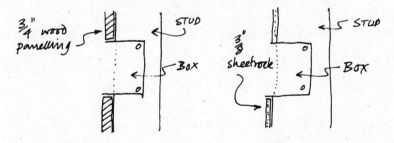

5. Recessed bathroom cabinets, medicine boxes, and vanities all require advance planning in order that the walls may be adequately framed to receive them—some are too wide to fit between studs 16″ on center.

After all this has been done—known as the roughing out—the electrician will contact the Underwriters Laboratory Inspector who will inspect everything, and if satisfactory will issue a certificate and notify the utility company who will then connect the power to the house. At this point you will have at least one outlet with power in the house.

Then the walls may be insulated and covered, and the electrician will wire all the different receptacles in the outlet boxes.

A DUPLEX
RECEPTACLE 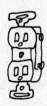    A SWITCH

When everything is complete another inspection must be made before the final certificate is issued. This certificate from the Underwriters Laboratory is required by banks for loans and mortgages, and insurance companies, so you must obtain it.

As well as the wiring described above there are other wiring jobs which should be planned at the roughing out stage. These include:

> Thermostat wiring for heaters
> Telephones may be pre-wired at this stage
> Antenna wiring & cable vision wiring
> Hi-fi speaker systems
> Intercoms
> Doorbells
> Central vacuuming systems
> Air conditioners
> Exhaust fans
> Fans for heatilater fireplaces

PLUMBING

While plumbing is not as inherently dangerous as electrical work, it can often cause greater inconvenience if improperly installed or, in cold areas, insufficiently insulated. Moreover, many communities forbid certain jobs to be done by anyone except a licensed plumber. While the purpose of this section is not to dissuade you from attempting your own plumbing, it does not explain the techniques or intricacies involved, but simply provides you with sufficient awareness of the various jobs to be able to plan your plumbing intelligently with the help of a professional plumber.

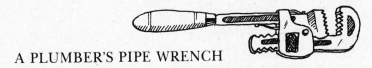

A PLUMBER'S PIPE WRENCH

The plumbing of a house consists of three main parts: getting the water to the house—**SUPPLY,** draining the water and waste from the house—**DRAINAGE,** and all the work in between—**FIXTURES.**

1. Supply.

The source of supply may be the public mains in urban areas, or private wells or springs in rural areas. The first will certainly have local codes and regulations attached, which if adhered to will ensure a proper and adequate supply. The second may not be governed by any ordinances at all, and it will be advisable to seek local professional advice.

Wells are the most common form of water supply in the country, although sometimes springs and running water may be used to advantage. Since most modern wells are drilled with specialized equipment that can penetrate even rock easily, the location of the well is often simply a matter of convenience to the well driller, but in areas where the sub strata is irregular it has often proved useful to employ a water dowser to determine where the well should be dug. A difference of a few feet may mean a substantial saving in drilling costs.

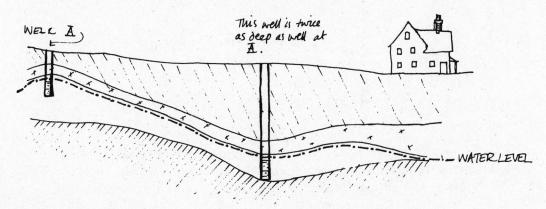

In general the well should be as close to the house as possible, and as far away from the disposal system as possible—and preferably uphill from it. Also, take into consideration the possibility of future disposal systems which future neighbors might install, and also the fact that presently uncontaminated sources of water may not always remain so—therefore locate your well at least 50′ away from any surface body of water.

Once the well is dug you should have it tested for purity, color, and taste. Very often local health codes mandate this, in any case it is rarely worth taking a chance. Find out whether the water is hard or soft. If it is hard you may want to install a water softener, for hard water is difficult to lather and can cause scaling and eventual clogging of pipes. Soft water, on the other hand, often tastes bad.

The amount of water needed depends on the size of the house (measured in terms of the number of bedrooms) and the size of your family. Average consumption may be anything from 50 to 100 gallons per day per person, and may be much more if washing machines and dishwashers etc. are used. The well driller will tell you when the well will produce sufficient for your needs.

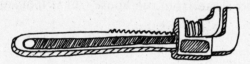

AN ADJUSTABLE WRENCH

In most cases a pump and pressure tank are required. Modern submersible pumps installed at the bottom of the well are electrically operated and so their installation must be coordinated with the electrician. Similarly, pressure tanks, which act as storage tanks and control the pump motor, are also electrically wired. The most important point here is to install a large enough tank so that the pump does not start operating every time a faucet is turned on.

A 42 GALLON PRESSURE TANK

The water may be piped to the house in metal or plastic pipe. Plastic is much cheaper but is sometimes prohibited by code. In either case the pipe should be buried carefully so that it will not be crushed by rocks and damaged.

Whatever else you do, make sure that this supply line is *ADEQUATELY INSU-LATED* if there is any danger of freezing weather in your area. This may be achieved by burying the line below the frost line, lagging (wrapping) it with insulating material or the judicious use of heat tape—electrically heated wire wrapped around the pipe. It doesn't matter how good the rest of your plumbing is if the supply line freezes in mid winter. Frozen pipes are expensive to thaw and can cause a lot of damage if they burst.

2. Drainage.

Once again, because drainage systems may vitally influence the health of the entire community, there are often stringent regulations governing such systems.

The best individual sewage system is the septic tank and drainage field. This consists of a house drain, a septic tank, an outlet sewer, a distribution box, and a disposal field.

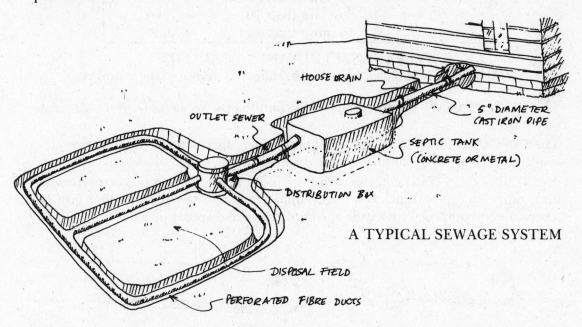

A TYPICAL SEWAGE SYSTEM

The location will be partly determined by the lay of the land—since the drainage should be preferably downhill and away from the water supply. But remember that you may need access to the septic tank in the event it needs servicing.

The SOIL PIPE is the main drain from the house to the septic tank. This is

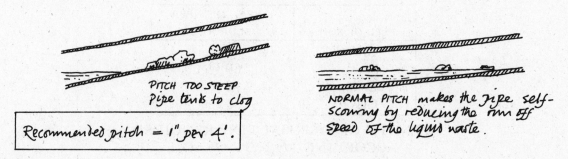

usually made from 5″ cast iron pipe and must be pitched at the right slope. If it is too steep waste will accumulate in the pipe.

The SEPTIC TANK is either tar-coated steel or concrete. Concrete costs more but lasts longer. The raw sewage enters the septic tank and bacterial action breaks the solids down into gases and liquids which drain off to the disposal field. The size of the tank is important, for a tank which is too small will soon become overloaded with sludge and may back up into the house.

NUMBER OF BEDROOMS	NUMBER OF PERSONS SERVED	CAPACITY OF SEPTIC TANK IN GALLONS
1 or 2	no more than 4	350
3	no more than 6	550
4	no more than 8	600
5	no more than 10	750
6	no more than 12	1,000

AVERAGE SEPTIC TANK CAPACITIES
(IMPORTANT: check local codes, they may require larger tanks)

The OUTLET SEWER is the pipe which connects the septic tank to the distribution box.

The DISTRIBUTION BOX is a small tank which distributes the liquids from the septic tank to the disposal lines of the disposal field.

The DISPOSAL FIELD consists of two or more lines of drain tile or perforated fibre pipe through which the sewage liquid seeps into the surrounding ground where it is decomposed by bacteria, completing the disposal process.

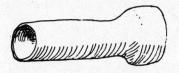

A SECTION OF CLAY
DRAINAGE TILE

A SECTION OF A LENGTH OF
PERFORATED FIBRE PIPE

The number and length of disposal lines depends on the size and occupancy of the house and the type of ground. For example, a large house on a clay site will

TYPE OF SOIL	LINEAL FEET PER BEDROOM
Gravel	40 feet
Sand	60 feet
Loam	90 feet
Clay	160 feet

LENGTH OF DISPOSAL LINE REQUIRED
ACCORDING TO TYPE OF SOIL

require much more disposal line than a small house in more porous ground such as sand.

The slope and size of the trenches to be dug for the disposal lines is also very important, and depends on the type of soil and the contour of the land. This is something which must be planned with the excavator who will dig all the holes and trenches; ideally, at the same time as the foundation is excavated.

The recommended slope is about 3″ per 100′. Individual lines should not be longer than 100′. At least two should be laid, even though less than 100′ is necessary—in case one line becomes temporarily waterlogged. The line should be about 18″ below ground, and if in non-porous soil it should be laid in a gravel filled trench, the whole being covered with a layer of straw or building paper to prevent clogging.

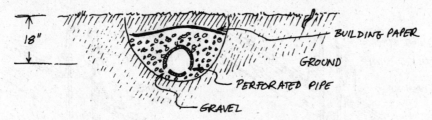

CROSS SECTION OF DISPOSAL TRENCH

Many houses use a separate tank for washing machines, as too much water in the solid waste tank might impair the bacteriological breakdown; not to mention the inhibiting factor of non-biodegradable detergents.

3. Fixtures.

Fixtures include sinks, tubs, showers, water closets * and even outside faucets. Planning with the plumber is the most important aspect of this work. The location of the water heater, the route the hot and cold water lines will take, adequate stopcocks and drain valves are among the things to be considered.

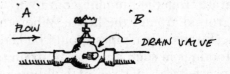

STOPCOCK (CONTROL VALVE, OR GATE VALVE)—when closed the flow of water is stopped completely.

STOP & DRAIN VALVE This valve can stop the flow as the stopcock does, but it can also allow the water from side "B" to drain from the drain valve.

It helps to keep as much of the plumbing as possible concentrated in one area of

---

* Usually called toilets by the layman; the plumber calls the whole room the toilet.

the house—hot water will cool off if it has to stand, or travel long distances between supply and outlet; the economy in piping achieved through careful planning may also be considerable. Every fixture should be able to be turned off independently, and the whole system should be capable of being drained easily.

Copper is still the best material to use, although better, and adequate, grades of plastic are being developed all the time, and plastic is much cheaper than copper.

One very important aspect to check on is that the whole system is adequately vented. This is necessary to prevent sewage gases from entering the house and to permit quick draining. Proper venting is all too often neglected, and is rather more complicated than merely installing one vent stack (pipe). Make sure that a competent plumber takes care of this. If the vent stack, or stacks pass through the roof, you will have to make sure they are flashed correctly, for this is a major source of roof leaks.

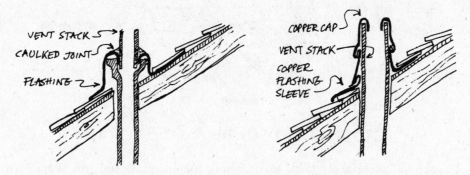

TWO METHODS OF FLASHING THE VENT STACK AT THE ROOF

The plumbing, like the wiring, should be roughed-out when the house has been framed so that all pipes and lines may be chased (built in) in the walls. This is another reason for planning ahead of time in consultation with the plumber.

Separate from the plumbing but to do with water, is the provision for drainage of the ground around the house. When the foundations are complete, drainage tile or perforated fiber pipes should be laid in a bed of gravel all around the base of the footings in such a way as to drain off to the lowest point. The gravel should be covered with a layer of building paper (to prevent clogging) and then the ground may be carefully back-filled to slope away from the house.

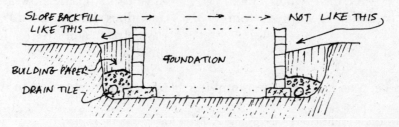

HEATING

Houses may be heated by electricity, hot water, hot air, kerosene, coal or firewood.

1. Coal and Wood.

The use of coal or wood requires either a fireplace or a stove. Wood (or coal) burning stoves can be very effective and economical, and, in fact, kept America warm for years. But they tend to be dirty and time consuming. It's all right if you only plan to use the house for weekend hunting trips, and like to chop wood, but for permanent living the inconvenience of getting up every six hours throughout the winter to stoke the stove cannot compare with the ease of merely adjusting a thermostat.

THE POT BELLY
WOOD STOVE

However, as an auxiliary system in case of a power failure, or just for the comfort and cheeriness of sitting around a glowing stove or an open fireplace, it is to be highly recommended. Iron stoves are relatively simply installed. Efficient fireplaces that give off heat and do not smoke the house out every time the wind changes direction require a lot of knowledge and skill to build. If you plan to have a fireplace employ an experienced mason, or study fireplace construction thoroughly first. You will need to understand such things as flue sizes, fire boxes,

the proper founding of hearths, the corbeling of smoke chambers and correct chimney dimensions.

2. Kerosene.

The use of kerosene space heaters is on the wane since they too can be dirty and are considered a fire hazard. Many insurance companies will not write policies for houses heated this way. However, if kept very clean and provided with an adequate chimney they are certainly efficient heat givers. The important thing about the chimney—as with all chimneys—is that it be at least 2' higher than the highest part of the roof in order to draw properly and not smoke you out.

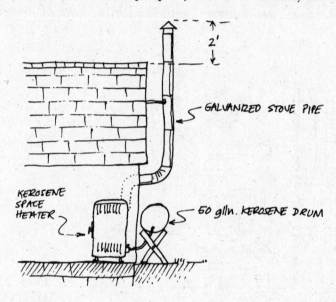

3. Gas.

Gas heat is not very efficient and is very expensive. Avoid it.

4. Electricity.

Electric baseboard heat is the cheapest automatic system to install since there is no ductwork, expensive furnace equipment or chimney involved. Every room may

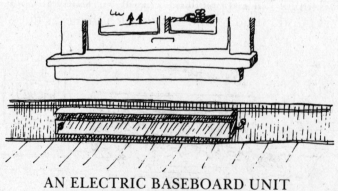

AN ELECTRIC BASEBOARD UNIT
INSTALLED UNDER A WINDOW

be separately controlled and it is a clean and silent form of heat BUT—the house must be insulated very well or otherwise the electricity bill will be enormous.

The baseboard units are normally installed under windows and are of various sizes. If you intend to use this kind of heat your electrician can advise you on the size and quantity of units necessary, and you should plan the location of shelves and closets accordingly, remembering that you will need a certain amount of clear wall space in every room.

5. Hot Water.

Hot water heat is often considered the most comfortable kind of heat. It requires a heating plant of some kind to heat the water—usually an oil-fired furnace—and a series of baseboard units similar to the electric units, although the hot water units are all connected whereas the electric units are separate. It is not a dry heat and so is very comfortable although the noise of the water running through the pipes may be annoying.

Radiators are another form of hot water heat—their main disadvantage being their size and the space they take up. Also you must take precautions against ever allowing the house to freeze, or the radiators will burst if not drained, which can cause a lot of damage.

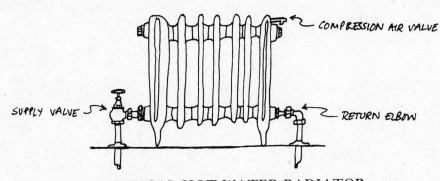

A TYPICAL HOT WATER RADIATOR

6. Hot Air.

Hot air heat is achieved by using a furnace to heat air which is forced through ducts and out of registers or grills in the floors or walls. This is the least conspicuous form of heat and if used with fiberglass duct work it can be very quiet, unlike the transatlantic liner noises often associated with metal ductwork. By using fiberglass, a humidifier and central air-conditioning may also be built into the system providing a very efficient and sophisticated form of "internal atmospheric control".

Both hot water and hot air systems should be planned and installed by qualified heating engineers—who are often also plumbers. The only carpentry involved is the installation of grills through which the heat passes—illustrated on the next page—and occasional provision for the ductwork.

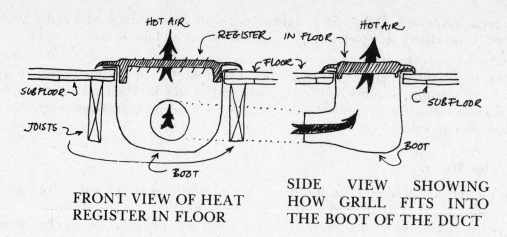

**FRONT VIEW OF HEAT
REGISTER IN FLOOR**

**SIDE VIEW SHOWING
HOW GRILL FITS INTO
THE BOOT OF THE DUCT**

Any heating system using a furnace will require a fuel tank to hold the oil which fires the furnace. It is always economical to have the largest one possible since fuel rates diminish the more you buy at one time. It may be possible to install the fuel tank in the basement or you may prefer to keep it outside the house. Tanks are made to hold 275 gallons, 500 gallons or 1,000 gallons and may be stood on the ground or buried conveniently underground with just the filling pipe sticking up. If burying the tank seems like the best idea (it is after all not a pretty object) plan this well in advance so that the necessary excavation may be performed with all the other excavating work.

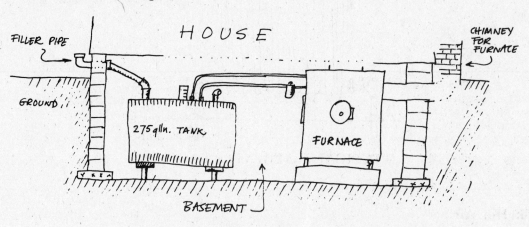

OIL TANK KEPT IN BASEMENT OR CRAWL SPACE

**1,000 GALLON OIL TANK BURIED FAR FROM HOUSE BUT
WITHIN EASY REACH OF THE LARGE OIL DELIVERY TRUCKS**

INSULATION

No matter what form of heat is used, the house will be much warmer if it is well insulated. Indeed, insulation works both ways and will not only keep the house warmer in winter, it will keep it cooler in summer. Thus it will save money on your heating bills *and* your electricity bills if you use air conditioning.

Thermal insulation is anything which prevents or reduces heat transference from one area to another, such as from the inside of a house to the outside. Every barrier between the inside and the outside has some insulating value, even the sheathing and the siding, but some materials have a much higher resistance than others. The insulating value of a material is referred to as its R factor—the higher the R factor, the better the insulation. Some idea of the difference between R factors may be gained by observing houses with approved insulating material in winter and houses without.

House A has no insulation and the heat from the building has escaped through the roof, melting the snow—but leaving snow at the eaves and rake overhangs, which are not exposed on the underneath to the building's heat. House B has lost no heat through the roof and the snow has remained, unmelted—and incidentally forming an extra layer of insulation.

Structural insulating board which may be used instead of sheathing is probably the cheapest form of insulation, although it has a relatively low R factor.

A comparatively new form of insulation is the use of different plastics—styrenes and urethanes, which are made in such a way as to trap hundreds of small air spaces within them—a dead air space being good insulation. Polystyrene, with the use of proper equipment, may be sprayed onto, or into, a building, and has the advantage of a high R factor in relation to its thickness. Other materials require a much greater thickness to attain the same R factor. It can also be obtained under various trade names in 4' x 8' and 2' x 8' sheets in thicknesses of ½" to 2" with R factors of 4 to 8 respectively.

Another form of insulation is the loose, granular kind, sold in sacks or bags, which is simply poured into the walls between studs. This is most often blown through holes drilled in the sides of existing buildings which were built without insulation. It may also be used in attic floors by pouring it between the attic joists.

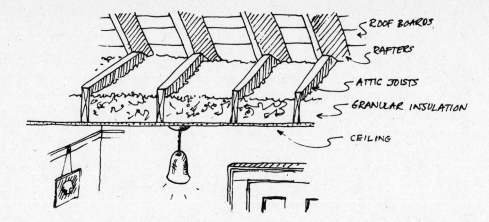

The commonest kind of insulation is strips of fiberglass. This is made in short lengths, called batts, or rolls, of varying thicknesses, widths and lengths. Both batts and rolls may also be obtained with a paper or aluminum foil backing. The backing increases the R factor somewhat, but its main purpose is to act as a vapor barrier, necessary to prevent condensation forming between the ceiling and the roof.

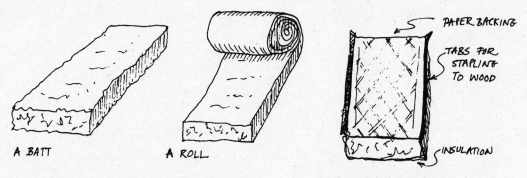

FIBERGLASS INSULATION   A PAPER BACKED PIECE OF
                               FIBERGLASS INSULATION

Since heat rises, the heat loss in a house is greatest through the roof, and least through the floors. Therefore there are different thicknesses of insulation for installation in the roof, walls and floors, each with a different R factor.

	THICKNESS	R FACTOR
Ceiling	6"–6½"	R19–R22
Walls	3"–3½"	R9 –R11
Floors	2"–2¼"	R6 –R7

TYPICAL THICKNESSES OF FIBERGLASS INSULATION,
THE RESPECTIVE R FACTOR, AND
WHERE IT SHOULD BE USED

Fiberglass rolls are made in 50′ and 100′ rolls, batts are commonly 4′ long. Both batts and rolls are made in various widths: 15″, 19″, and 23″, designed to fit between framing members 16″ and 24″ on center.

Backed insulation should be applied with the backing toward the interior of the house; it is commonly either stapled flush with the framing members, or recessed ¾″ to 1″, thus providing the extra insulation of a dead air space when the finish wall (or ceiling) is applied.

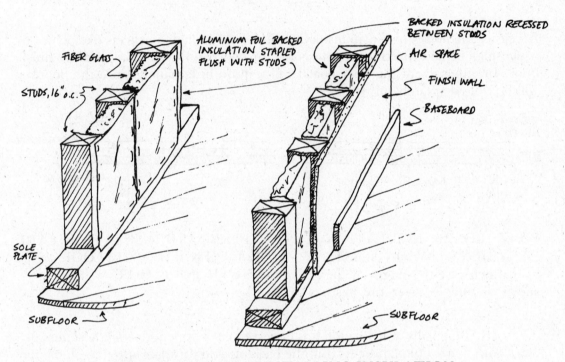

TWO METHODS OF INSTALLING INSULATION

Another way of insulating which sometimes saves time and money is to use unbacked batts, and sheets of plastic. The batts are simply wedged into place be-

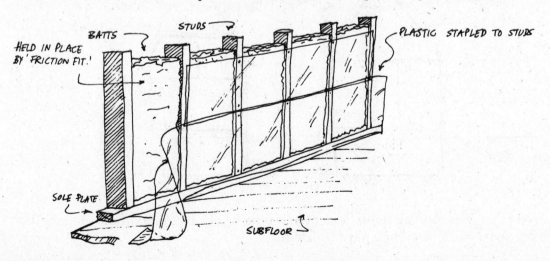

tween the studs or rafters, needing no staples to hold them, and then plastic is tacked over the whole to form the vapor barrier.

Floors may be insulated with fiberglass as shown below:

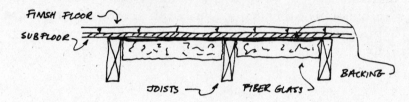

An easier method is to use an insulating fiber board, made in sheets like plywood, which may be laid directly over the joists, or between the subfloor and the finish floor. In either event the fiber board will require little nailing since the flooring will hold it adequately in place.

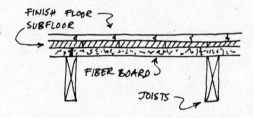
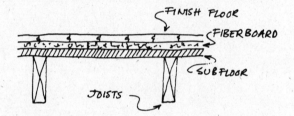

FIBER BOARD INSULATION LAID DIRECTLY ON JOISTS —in which case the edges of the sheets should lie over the joists

FIBERBOARD INSULATION LAID BETWEEN THE SUBFLOOR AND THE FINISH FLOOR

If you are using rolls of insulation it is easiest to cut it to length *before* installing it. Cut it with a mat knife and cut from the backing side. Insulate *after* the plumbing and wiring have been roughed in.

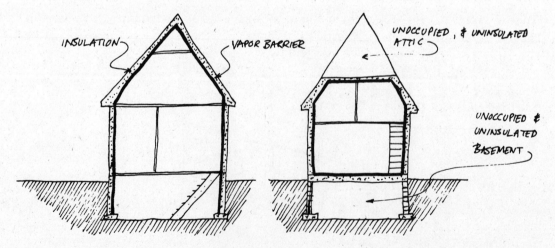

Whether you insulate the basement and attic or not is unimportant—but the living space must be completely insulated.

VENTILATION

If a house is warm inside and cold outside, and there is sufficient humidity within the house, this humidity will condense on contact with the cold surface of the house. This is usually most noticeable at the roof. Similarly, cold and damp air rising from the ground underneath the house will condense on contact with the floor joists. All this moisture would eventually cause the wood to rot, so steps should be taken to prevent condensation from occurring. This is achieved by ventilating adequately all parts of the building where condensation is likely to occur.

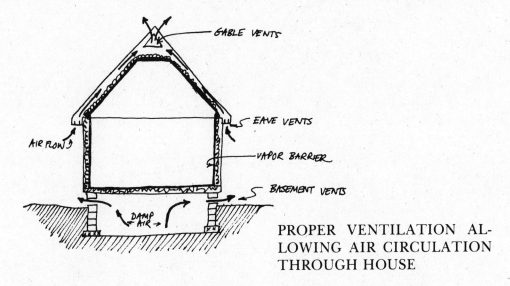

PROPER VENTILATION ALLOWING AIR CIRCULATION THROUGH HOUSE

In the basement, or crawl space, ventilation is achieved by providing vents in the foundation walls as described in chapter 1.

In the roof—the other main danger area—even when a vapor barrier has been used, condensation may still occur, so all parts of the roof behind the insulation should be thoroughly ventilated. Here, all that needs to be done is to provide for an air flow between the rafters, under the sheathing and behind the insulation.

At the eaves this is done by drilling holes and inserting screened louvers—as explained in chapter 4. At the ridge the easiest way is to pull the insulation down into the attic floor and vent the remaining area (above the attic floor) by means of louvered vents in the gables.

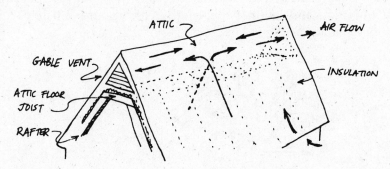

The vents for the gable may be made of aluminum. Lumberyards usually carry a good selection of different shapes and sizes. They are mostly flanged to fit simply into a hole cut in the siding the same size.

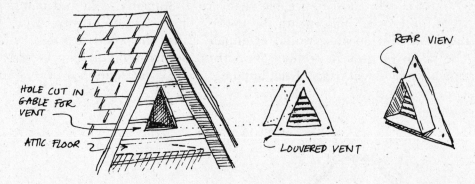

It is also possible to use small wooden louvered shutters or louvered doors and make a window frame, as described in the next chapter, and insert this.

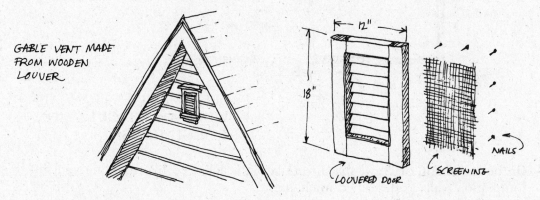

If you make the louver yourself from a shutter, do not forget to tack some wire screening to the back to keep out the wasps and other insects.—The aluminum factory-made louvers have the screening already in.

If you plan to use all the roof space inside, right up to the ridge, and do not want even the smallest attic floor, then somehow you must allow the air rising up between each rafter to circulate, for venting only at the eaves allows air to enter but does not provide for a free flow—and condensation will result. There are factory built aluminum ridge vents which may be installed when the roof is being sheathed, or you may build your own, as shown below. But the best method for a house with fiberglass insulation between the rafters and finished ceilings is to allow for an attic space at the ridge.

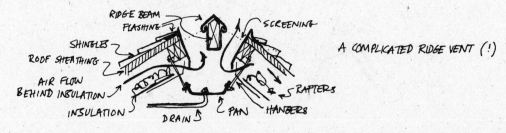

BACKFILLING

Backfilling is the filling in or covering over of all the excavation which may be necessary. There are so many different things to be dug or backfilled that it is a good idea to list everything in one place.

You will need the excavator for the following holes and ditches—all of which may be dug at one time (and all backfilled at one time) if you plan everything far enough ahead:

1. The main excavation for the foundation. (Below the frostline.)

2. The trench to the septic tank. (18″)

3. The hole for the septic tank. (Deep enough so the septic tank, whatever size it is, may be covered by a foot or so of earth.)

4. The trenches for the disposal lines. (18″)

5. The trench for the electric power line—if you decide to have underground wires. (18″—but remember they must be in metal conduit if they pass under a driveway.)

6. The telephone wires may be installed in the same trench as the power line.

7. The trench from the water supply to the house, which will contain not only the water line but the electrical wiring for the pump. (Below the frost line—this is very important if you don't want to dig it up every winter.)

8. A hole for any fuel tank you may want to bury—oil or gas. (Below ground but with the filler pipe above ground!)

9. A trench for the fuel line from the tank to the house. (18″)

10. A run off ditch for any foundation drainage.

11. Trenches for any culverts * that may be necessary under the driveway.

---

* A culvert is a pipe large enough to carry a stream under a driveway. If you need culverts remember to buy them on the basis of the size of the stream when it has most water flowing—many streams big enough to wash away a driveway dry up completely sometimes.

It may well help, before you start to build, to draw a sketch of the building site and show the proposed location of everything on it as in the sketch below. Not only may the local building code require one, but it will help you organize the work better, and eliminate the possibility of forgetting something.

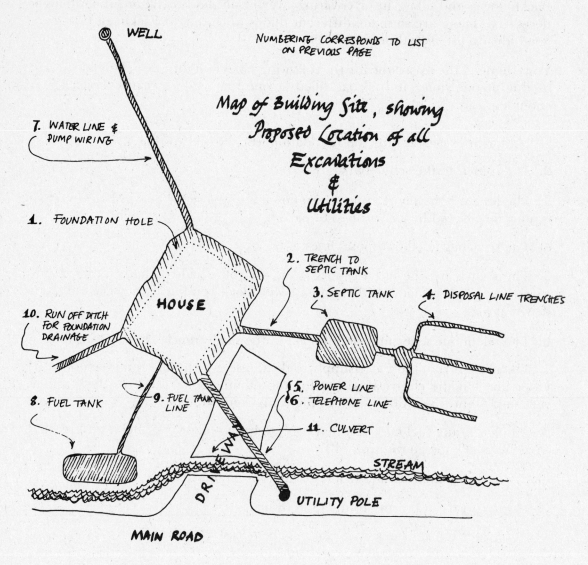

NUMBERING CORRESPONDS TO LIST
ON PREVIOUS PAGE

Map of Building Site, showing
Proposed Location of all
Excavations
&
Utilities

WELL

7. WATER LINE & PUMP WIRING

1. FOUNDATION HOLE

2. TRENCH TO SEPTIC TANK

3. SEPTIC TANK

4. DISPOSAL LINE TRENCHES

HOUSE

10. RUN OFF DITCH FOR FOUNDATION DRAINAGE

5. POWER LINE
6. TELEPHONE LINE

8. FUEL TANK

9. FUEL TANK LINE

11. CULVERT

STREAM

DRIVEWAY

UTILITY POLE

MAIN ROAD

BIBLIOGRAPHY

NAHB Research Foundation, INSULATION MANUAL: HOMES, APART-MENTS. Rockville, Maryland: National Association of Home Builders, 1971

Probably the best and most definitive manual on insulation yet published. All the facts and figures.

National Lumber Manufacturers Association, INSULATION OF WOOD-FRAME STRUCTURES. Washington: National Forest Products Association, 1964

Contains useful maps and illustrations and a full bibliography of books on insulation.

Nowack, John F., ELECTRICAL WORK, A HANDBOOK OF TOOLS, MATE-RIALS, METHODS, AND DIRECTIONS. New York: D. Van Nostrand Co., 1945

An easy to read introduction to electricity in the home.

NATIONAL ELECTRICAL CODE, Chicago: National Board of Fire Under-writers.

The complete legal specifications for all types of electrical work.

Schaefer, Carl T., and Smith, Robert E., HOME MECHANICS. Milwaukee: The Bruce Publishing Co., 1961

A useful book for understanding the basic principles and maintainance of "the works".

Wolf, Ralph T., THE WISE HANDBOOK OF HOME PLUMBING. New York: Wm. H. Wise & Co., 1953

A well illustrated basic guide to all aspects of home plumbing.

As well as customs and ceremonies associated with housebuilding, there are also many time-honored tricks played by tradesmen to ensure payment. One such trick was the mason's habit of building a pane of glass across the chimney, high up in the flue. The glass being clear, no obstruction could be seen, but the fire would not draw until the mason was paid—when he would then simply drop a brick down the chimney!

Paying the Mason

CHAPTER SEVEN. *Interior Finish*

The interior finish of the house consists of installing the windows and doors, covering the ceilings and walls, and laying the floors.

1. Windows.

Windows may be divided into three classes: 1. Fixed Windows—which do not open; 2. Casement Windows—which open by having one side hinged to any side of the frame; they may open inwards or outwards, and be hinged from the top, sides or bottom; and 3. Sash Windows—which open by sliding up or down and are held open (or closed) by friction, pins or counterweights. (There are also sideways sliders.)

Theoretically the fixed window is not really a window since the origin of the word implies a hole through which not only light but air may pass. Saxon buildings had no chimneys—merely a hole in the wall or roof—the "wind eye"—through which the smoke escaped and fresh air came in.

All kinds of windows may be bought as ready made units from a number of manufacturers, in many different shapes, styles and sizes. All that needs to be done is to order the right size, place it in the rough opening, and when the inside walls are covered and the outside walls are sheathed, secure the window in place by nailing the trim (or casing) to the window frame and the inside and outside walls.

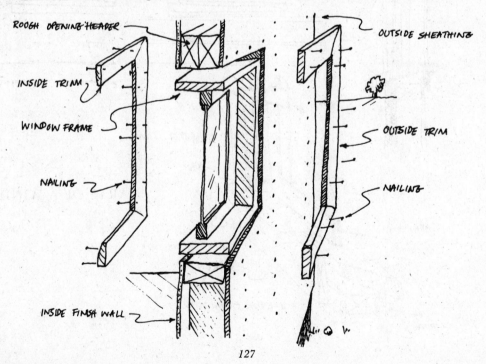

Such units often have many advantages: they come complete, with storm sash for extra insulation in cold climates, and screens for the insect-laden summer months; all the hardware is affixed—hinges, handles, locks, etc.; and they are quick and easy to install.

The alternative is to buy sash—the part of the window that actually holds the glass—and make your own frames. This has the advantage of being much cheaper, and gives you the opportunity to tailor each window to your particular needs without sacrificing any quality control.

A third possibility is to obtain complete or partial second-hand units from breakers' yards, old houses being torn down, auctions or second-hand building supply yards. There are many such places, and the materials thus obtained are very often superior in quality, if sometimes less sophisticated, and far cheaper than can be bought new.

If you decide, for reasons of economy or quality, to make your own window frames, the simplest form to make is an outward opening casement window. This consists of the following parts:

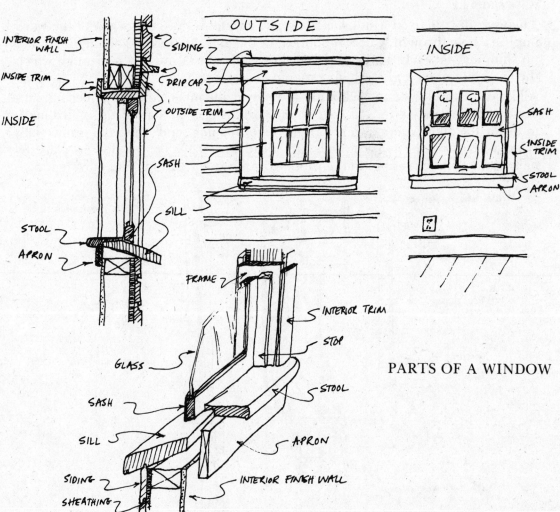

PARTS OF A WINDOW

Again, the sash is the part which holds the glass—if there are lots of panes of glass in the sash, it is described as a 6 light, 9 light or 12 light window according to however many panes there are. The frame is the part that holds the sash, and the trim (or casing) is the part that holds the frame in the wall.

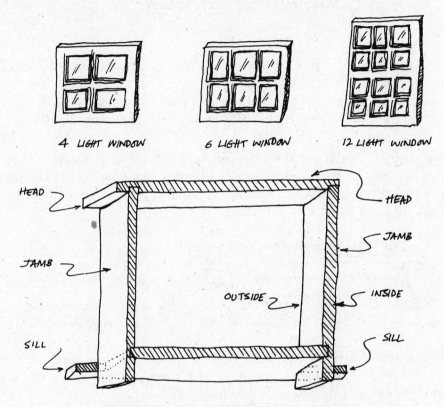

PARTS OF A WINDOW FRAME

MAKING THE FRAME & TRIM FOR
A CASEMENT WINDOW:

1. Measure the width of the rough opening, i.e. "x" in the illustration below.

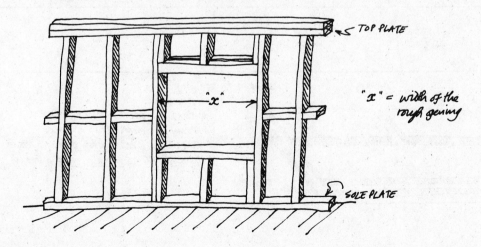

2. Cut a piece of ⁵/₄″ thick lumber as shown below: (This is the head.)

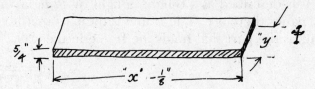

The length should be the measurement "x" from the rough opening less ⅛″ so that it will fit easily.

The width, "y", equals the width of the studs, plus the thickness of the exterior sheathing and the interior finish wall plus another ⅛″ for irregularities.

3. Cut two dadoes *, each the thickness of the jambs. The jambs too, should be made from ⁵/₄″ thick lumber, so the dadoes will be about 1³/₁₆″ wide—but measure your wood, for the thickness of nominal ⁵/₄″ lumber varies from lumberyard to lumberyard, and you want a snug joint.

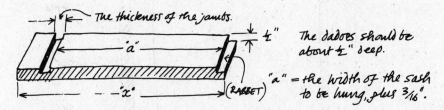

Make the first dado (actually a rabbet) at the end you want to hinge the sash. If the framing stud on this side is straight and plumb you will make the window extra strong by fixing the jamb with the hinges to it.

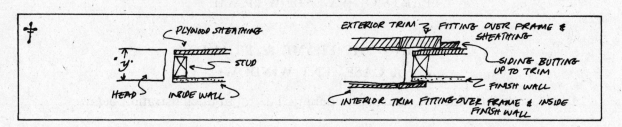

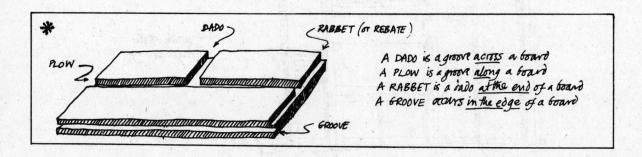

To make a dado mark the edges of it carefully first and then make several saw-cuts across the board, as shown at "a", and then chisel away the dado making the bottom as smooth as possible.

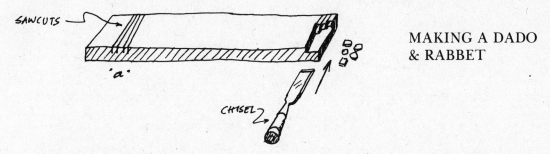

MAKING A DADO
& RABBET

A circular saw is easiest if you can set the depth of the blade (or the height of a table saw blade). (A "dado head set"—a special combination of blades for power saws—is easiest and quickest, but not really worth the time involved in setting it up if you only have one or two to cut.)

Pre-electric carpenters had planes with irons (blades) of varying widths which could be set to the required depth. However, even they most usually simply used a back saw and a chisel.

4. When the head of the frame is ready, the two jambs must be cut, and dadoed to receive the sill.

To allow water to run off, the sill should slope downwards toward the outside at about an angle of 15°. For a close fit when shut, the bottom of the sash should also be trimmed to a 15° angle.

SHOWING   ANGLE
OF SILL & BOTTOM
OF SASH

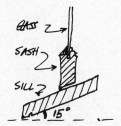

Use the bevel square set at 15°
to mark all the cuts involving
this slope.

As the window is to open outwards the sash is hinged to the outside edge of the jamb. So measure in from the outside edge of the jamb the thickness of the sash and draw a line parallel to the edge on the jamb.

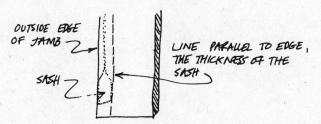

5. Fit the jamb into the dado in the head and measure off the height of the sash along this line, plus ¼″ for clearance of the sash while it is being opened and closed. Draw a line at 15° across the jamb to intersect this point and you have the top edge of the dado to receive the sill, as shown.

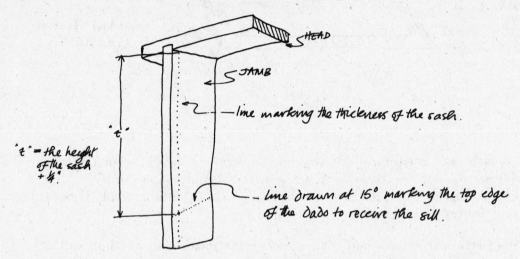

6. Measure the exact thickness of the sill—it may be made from ⁵/₄″, but better windows usually use 2″ stock—and mark off this thickness below the first line and cut the dado as for the head. Do this for both jambs and you have:

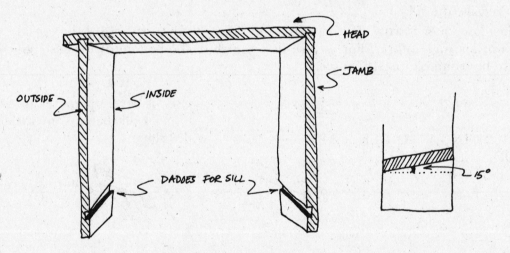

7. Cut off the bottom of the jambs so that the frame will fit easily into the rough

THE DADO
MOLDING PLANE

End View of a Left-
Handed Dado Plane

opening (with ½" or so to spare—so that one side or the other may be shimmed up if the opening is not perfectly square).

8. Now cut the sill as shown:

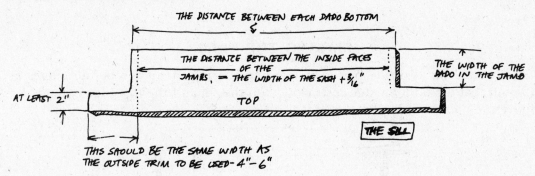

THE DISTANCE BETWEEN EACH DADO BOTTOM

THE DISTANCE BETWEEN THE INSIDE FACES OF THE JAMBS, = THE WIDTH OF THE SASH + ³⁄₁₆"

TOP

THE WIDTH OF THE DADO IN THE JAMB

AT LEAST 2"

THE SILL

THIS SHOULD BE THE SAME WIDTH AS THE OUTSIDE TRIM TO BE USED— 4"–6"

9. The back of the sill must now be cut at a 15° angle to be vertical, and a groove cut under the front edge to act as a drip edge. This groove is most easily cut by running the electric saw along, ¼" in from the edge, with the blade set ¼" deep.

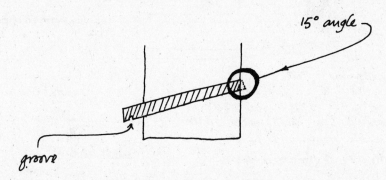

15° angle

groove

10. Now all four sides of the frame are complete and the whole thing should be nailed together and placed in the rough opening, taking care to see that it is as square as possible—or the sash will not fit.

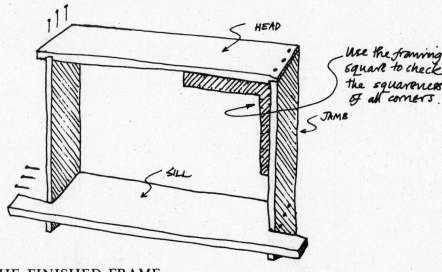

HEAD

Use the framing square to check the squareness of all corners.

JAMB

SILL

THE FINISHED FRAME

The frame is held in place by nailing the outside trim to the edges of the frame and to the studs comprising the rough opening (through the sheathing). But first, the building paper should come to the edge of the frame as explained in chapter 3.

MAKING THE TRIM

Cut and nail the two side pieces first—remembering to cut the bottom edges at 15°—so that the bottom edge rests closely on the sill and the top edge extends ¼" above the bottom of the head.

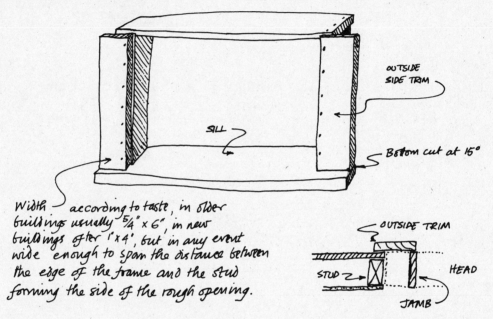

Then the top piece (architrave) is cut, its length being the distance from the outside edge of one trim to the other. On the top edge of this is nailed a piece of drip cap the same length.

FINISHED TRIM OUTSIDE SHOWING NAIL-ING—WHICH SHOULD BE SET AND FILLED AS IS THE SIDING (see chapter 4).

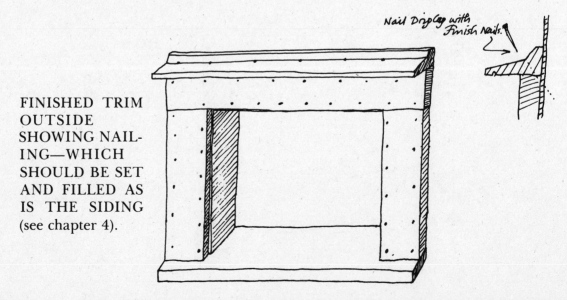

The inside trims, fitted after the walls are finished, are fitted in the same order, with the exception of the drip cap, and the addition of two extra pieces called the stool, and, inside, level, sill, and the apron—essentially the bottom piece of trim which also helps support the stool.

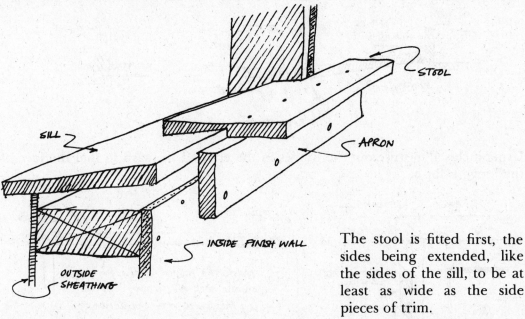

The stool is fitted first, the sides being extended, like the sides of the sill, to be at least as wide as the side pieces of trim.

Then the apron is cut the same length (or 1″ shorter) and nailed firmly under the stool. Finally the side pieces and the top piece are cut and nailed. The inside trim is more usually 1″ x 4″ and so need only be nailed with 8d. finish nails. Most lumberyards also carry interior window casing to be used as trim. A common variety is the Clamshell pattern:

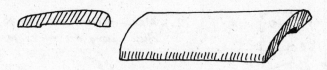

This is also used to trim the insides of door frames. The corners should be mitered.

With the frame built, and the trim holding it square and secure, the next step is to hang the window. Remember the sash should fit into the opening with a little clearance (⅛″) all round, and that the bottom should be beveled to match the angle of the sill slope. Also, the inside edge of the side opposite the hinges should be beveled slightly to allow the window to close and not leave too big a gap.

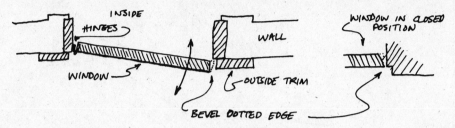

Using a chisel, mortise out the hinges in the edge of the sash so that the face of the hinge is flush.

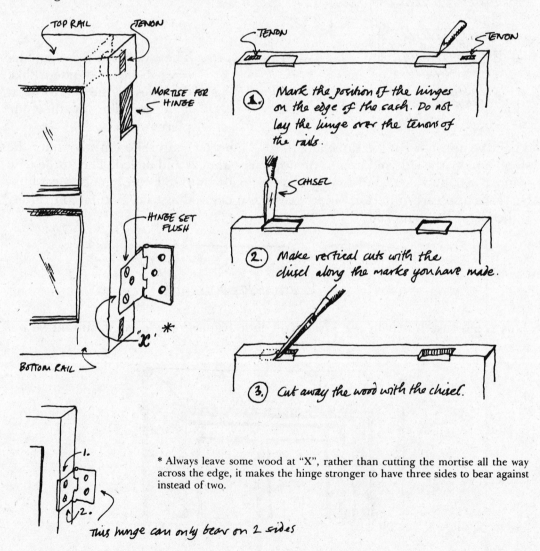

1. Mark the position of the hinges on the edge of the sash. Do not lay the hinge over the tenons of the rails.

2. Make vertical cuts with the chisel along the marks you have made.

3. Cut away the wood with the chisel.

* Always leave some wood at "X", rather than cutting the mortise all the way across the edge, it makes the hinge stronger to have three sides to bear against instead of two.

This hinge can only bear on 2 sides

With both hinges screwed to the sash, hold that sash in the frame and mark the position of the hinges on the frame—the outside of the sash being flush with the outside edge of the frame—cut out the hinge mortises in the frame, and screw everything together. To make life easier, it is possible to buy "loose pin" butts (hinges that come apart). Using this kind you can screw both parts of the hinge to the sash and the frame separately.

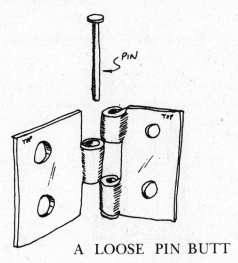

A LOOSE PIN BUTT

When the sash is hung, the only job that remains is to make the stop. The stop is the strip which runs around the inside of the frame, and against which the window closes. If you have built a stool, this serves as the bottom stop. Stop molding may be bought at lumberyards, or for something more substantial you may use some 1" x 2".

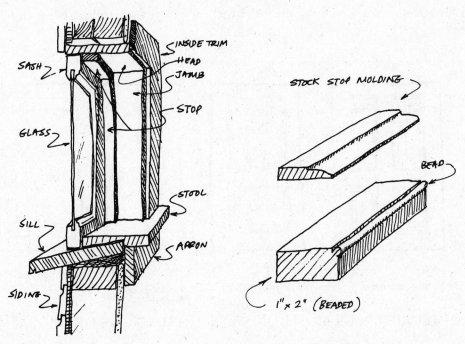

2. Doors.

Much of what has been said about windows can be said about doors. They too may be bought as units, complete with frame, casing, and sill; or old doors may be obtained, much more cheaply, and be framed in essentially the same manner as casement windows.

Some important points and differences to note are:

1. Exterior doors should open inwards, so that storm doors and screen doors may be hung to open outwards.

2. Sills should be made of oak (or some other HARD wood) which are available in standard dimensions to fit most doors, at lumberyards.

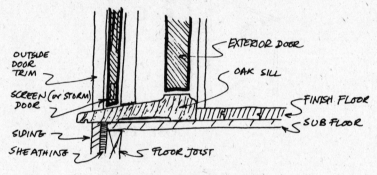

DETAIL OF DOOR SILL

3. Interior doors may be hung on which ever side, and to open inwards or outwards as convenience dictates. They are generally lighter and smaller than exterior doors and are trimmed the same on both sides.

4. Full length doors are usually hung with three hinges to prevent warping and sagging.

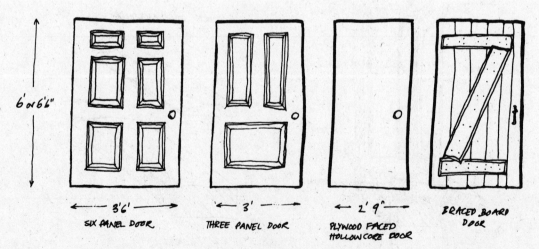

SOME DIFFERENT COMMON SIZES AND DESIGNS OF DOORS

3. Ceilings and Walls.

Ceilings and walls may be finished in a number of different ways, including plastering, panelling with wood or plywood, using various composition boards, or most commonly using gypsum board which may be either painted or papered.

1. Plastering is still one of the best ways of finishing quality houses although it is relatively expensive and requires a lot of skill—in fact, proper plastering is a trade in itself.

2. Plywood is made for interior use in a large variety of veneers and patterns. It too is very expensive but has the advantage of being very quickly applied compared with plastering which may require long periods to cure (dry). It is usually made to imitate vertical wood panelling and is usually applied vertically (on the walls). Care must be taken to ensure that all sheets are plumb and fitted tightly together, and that there is adequate nailing along all edges.

3. Wood panelling requires a high level of carpentry skill although it is relatively straightforward to cover wall surfaces with matched boards, and tongue and grooved knotty pine panelling is very popular.

SECTION OF WOOD WALL PANELLING AROUND A FIREPLACE

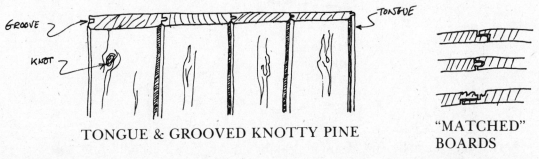

TONGUE & GROOVED KNOTTY PINE

"MATCHED" BOARDS

4. Gypsum board—more usually called Sheetrock, and sometimes plasterboard— is a material made in various thicknesses, and sheets 4′ x 8′, 4′ x 10′ and 4′ x 12′, consisting of a gypsum filler sandwiched between layers of paper. The edges are recessed to receive the joint compound which covers the edges.

Assuming the walls are framed with studs 16″ on center, ⅜″ thick sheets may be used, although ½″ thick sheets are better insulation, more fireproof, more rigid and less likely to bend.

If the whole interior is to be sheetrocked, the ceilings should be done first, nailing every 6″ to every framing member (second floor joists or rafters), with all joints centered over wood—as with sheets of plywood. Use 5d. cement-coated nails, or special Sheetrock nails which have flat heads and rings on the shanks to prevent them from pulling out. Or use two nails at a time, driven in at opposing angles.

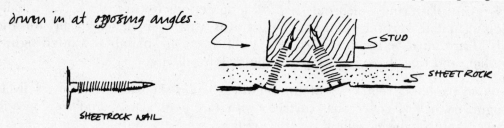

Hammer the nails in just below the surface so that the resulting indentation may be filled with spackle (joint compound) and then sanded smooth.

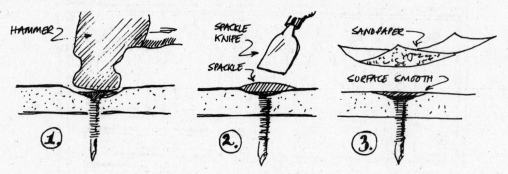

Joint compound is most economically bought in 5 gallon cans, although it is possible to buy it in ½ pint cans.

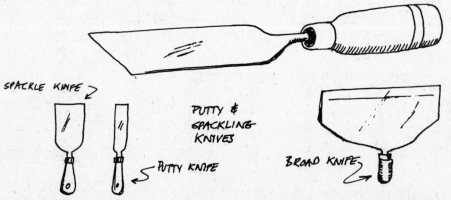

When sheets must be cut, draw a straight line, or snap a chalk line, and score along this line with a mat knife, then fold the Sheetrock away from the cut and make another cut in the **V** thus formed.

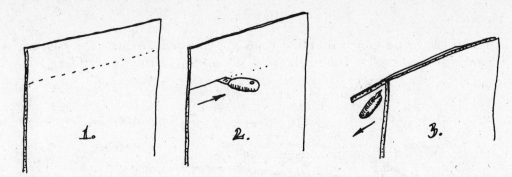

1.   2.   3.

After the ceiling has been covered, do the walls, using the sheets vertically or horizontally, which ever way involves least cutting and fewest joints. Try to keep the joints tight, especially in the corners, but do not worry about the edge at the floor, since the baseboard covers this.

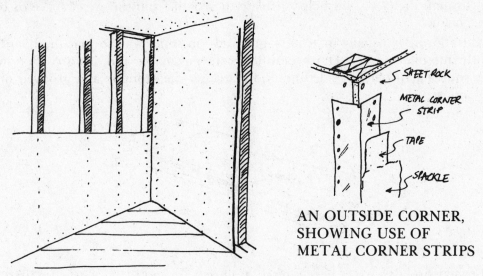

AN OUTSIDE CORNER,
SHOWING USE OF
METAL CORNER STRIPS

SHEET ROCK
METAL CORNER STRIP
TAPE
SPACKLE

When all the sheets are nailed in place the nail holes must be spackled and the joints taped.

First spread a layer of spackle along the joint, then press the tape over the crack and spread some more spackle over the whole, using a broad knife to feather the edges.

Allow this to dry, at least 24 hrs., sand smooth and repeat until the joint is perfectly smooth.

When taping in the corners, fold the tape first so that it fits more easily into the corner.

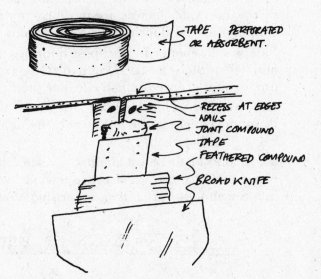

TAPE, PERFORATED OR ABSORBENT.
RECESS AT EDGES
NAILS
JOINT COMPOUND
TAPE
FEATHERED COMPOUND
BROAD KNIFE

4. Floors.

This is the last to be done, after the walls are finished, because the baseboard, which runs around the bottom of the wall, sits on top of the finish floor.

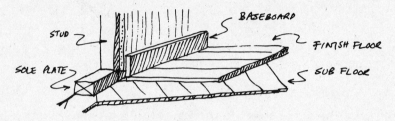

The first thing to ensure is that the subfloor is well nailed, level and clean. Then a layer of building paper is applied over the whole surface; this prevents dust passing through the floor and helps insulate the room from the crawl space or basement below.

Wood flooring is usually matched—grooved—in some way so that the boards fit tightly into one another. Hardwood floors such as maple and oak are often made with short narrow strips, side and end matched—i.e., tongue and grooved on all four sides.

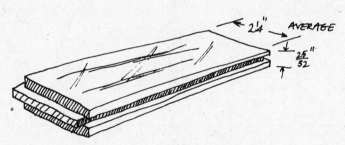

Other hardwoods such as beech, birch, walnut, ash, and hickory are also used, but more rarely. Hardwood floors are best since they wear longer, but pine, fir and hemlock—classed as softwoods—are also common flooring materials since they are considerably cheaper. These are also manufactured in matched, narrow pieces, but wider boards are more common. Indeed, in older houses it is not uncommon to find floorboards made of pine up to 18″ in width.

Pine is still among the cheapest floorings, and random width pine boards (6″, 8″ and 10″ wide) may be bought directly from sawmills, milled on one side, and tongue and grooved, much cheaper than packaged hardwood floors.

However, the wider the board, the more subject it is to expansion and contraction through changes in the moisture content, and this can result in unsightly gaps between floorboards.

Thus, one of the most important elements in obtaining lumber for flooring is being sure that the wood is properly dried. Green, unseasoned wood will shrink in a few months, often by a surprising amount.

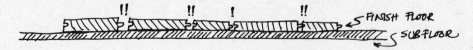

The direction the floorboards should run may be determined by any, or ideally but rarely all, of the following:

1. The boards should lie at right angles to the joists.

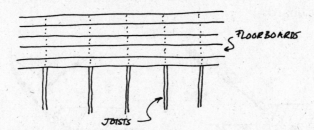

2. The boards should lie at right angles to the subfloor—or at 45° if the subfloor has been laid diagonally.

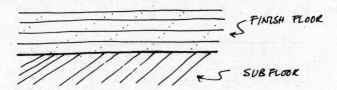

3. The boards often look best if laid lengthwise along the room.

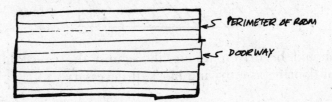

Having decided which way the boards are to run, start by placing the grooved edge against one wall and nailing through the top and tongue as shown, preferably into a joist.

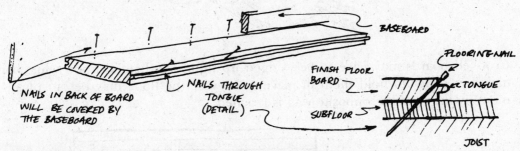

It will make it a lot easier to nail into the joists if you mark with chalk where they are on the building paper as you lay it down.

If you want to avoid a squeaky floor, use nails long enough to penetrate the tongue of the board, the paper, the subfloor and the joist below, as shown on the previous page.

To avoid damaging the edges of the boards when driving the nails, use a nailset as shown. However, leaving a fraction of the nail projecting provides an added grip for the next board.

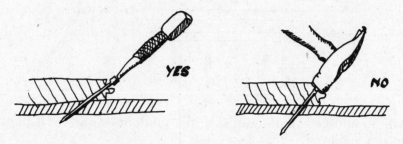

In nailing subsequent boards—be they the narrow strips or wide boards—make sure that all butt joints are well staggered.

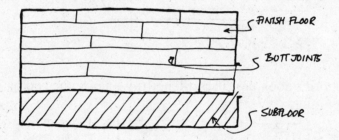

All boards should be driven up tightly against the preceding board, using a scrap piece of flooring as a driving block, if necessary.

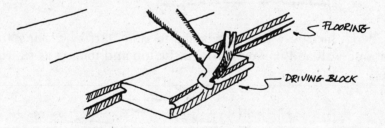

Crooked boards may have to be wedged up tightly and stood upon while being nailed in order to hold them in place; otherwise the floor may be out of alignment by the time the opposite wall is reached.

The secret of getting the last few boards down tightly lies in not nailing them! Fit them together, buckled, and then press them into place by standing on them.

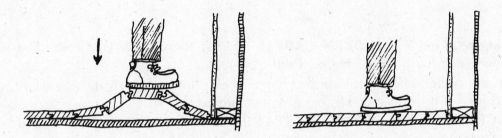

When the floor is fully laid the door trim should be made, fitting snugly to the floor, and then all thresholds and saddles should be nailed in place where different floors meet in doorways.

The baseboard is the last piece of trim to be made. This may be anything from a small piece of 1″ x 2″ to an elegantly molded baseboard as much as 12″ high.

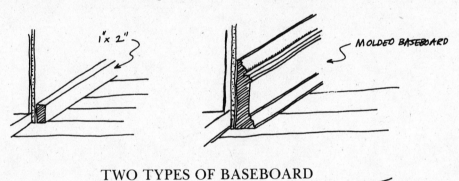

TWO TYPES OF BASEBOARD

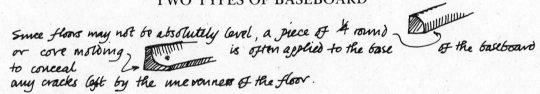

Since floors may not be absolutely level, a piece of ¼ round or cove molding is often applied to the base of the baseboard to conceal any cracks left by the unevenness of the floor.

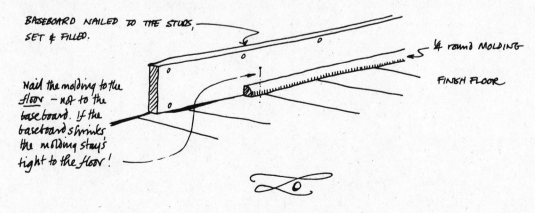

BASEBOARD NAILED TO THE STUDS, SET & FILLED.

¼ round MOLDING

FINISH FLOOR

Nail the molding to the floor — not to the baseboard. If the baseboard shrinks the molding stays tight to the floor!

BIBLIOGRAPHY

Hodgson, Fred T., MODERN CARPENTRY: A PRACTICAL MANUAL. Chicago: Frederick J. Drake & Co., 1909
An old, but excellent book on interior and exterior trim with detailed working drawings of doors, windows, cornices and staircases.

ARCHITECTURAL GRAPHIC STANDARDS (see bibliography at end of chapter 1.)

THE MODERN CARPENTER JOINER AND CABINET MAKER (see bibliography at end of chapter 2.)

CARPENTERS AND BUILDERS LIBRARY (see bibliography at end of chapter 1.)

APPENDIX

ESSENTIAL RED TAPE

Even someone already owning their own land is unlikely to be allowed to build willy-nilly without at least some red tape involved. So for those people, and others who do not even own land at all, this appendix is written. It covers briefly the main legal obstacles which will be encountered by the house builder.

Firstly, in securing land, there are TITLE SEARCHES, SURVEYS, and DEEDS to be made. Then there may be BUILDING CODES and ZONING LAWS to be considered, BUILDING PERMITS to be applied for, and HEALTH CERTIFI-CATES and CERTIFICATES OF OCCUPANCY to be obtained. Finally, on the financial side, there are LOANS, MORTGAGES, INSURANCES, ASSESS-MENTS and TAXES to work out.

The Land

Becoming a land owner involves a little more than merely handing over some money and receiving a deed. Of course, circumstances vary, but the process is basically as follows:

1. Engage a lawyer, for there is a lot of paperwork to be done, most of it legally complicated.

2. A survey of the land involved is made, preferably by a licensed surveyor, sometimes at the buyer's expense, sometimes the seller's, or sometimes shared.

3. The lawyer will make a title search to discover that there are no liens against the property, no taxes outstanding and what, if any, restrictions exist as to the use of the land.

4. Then a deed for the land is drawn up, and sometimes a contract covering the terms of the sale as well. Deeds vary from weak—"Quit Claim Deeds"—which merely divest the grantor (the party selling the land) of all claim to the land, to strong—"Warranty Deeds"—which assure the grantee (the party buying the land) of full legal possession and inurement from all "encumbrances."

5. Finally, with much stamping and signing of papers, the deed is filed with the county clerk, or his equivalent.

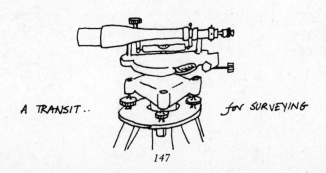

A TRANSIT.. _for_ SURVEYING

The Building

When the land is yours you may start to build, but you should be aware of the following possible restrictions and requirements—in fact, you should investigate these when you are considering buying the land, or you may find—after you have bought your future estate—that the local government forbids three-story thatched towers, or whatever you were planning to build.

1. Zoning Laws.

Many areas have zoning laws which govern the amount of land on which a house may be built, how near it may be built to the boundaries, what materials may be used, and many other aspects of building. Most agencies however may be approached for "variances," but this is something a lawyer is useful for.

2. Building Codes.

There may be a variety of building codes in force, ranging from state to local, which must be complied with. These sometimes set detailed standards for construction. Some areas require plumbing to be done only by licensed plumbers, and almost no power company will connect electricity without an inspection. Copies of applicable codes may usually be obtained from Town Halls or County Office Buildings.

3. Building Permits.

Some areas require that you obtain a building permit before construction may begin. This is generally to ensure that local building codes and/or zoning laws are being complied with. Where building permits are required it is also often necessary to apply for Certificates of Occupancy when the building is completed.

4. Health Certificates.

Submission of sewage disposal plans and water supply details is often required at the county level, and sometimes at the town or village level. Inspections may be made and tests conducted to see if everything satisfies local sanitation requirements.

All of the above may be readily discovered by application at local government offices, and should be thoroughly investigated *before* you start to build.

The Money

Money is needed to build the house and, just as important, to pay taxes on it after it is complete. How the money is raised to build depends on you, but the taxes are established, and you should be aware of their extent before you start.

The land is usually bought outright from the seller, and if necessary financed by a PERSONAL LOAN. This is something either your lawyer, or the broker managing the sale, will be able to advise you on.

MORTGAGES are usually only given on buildings already existing, and should not be confused with BUILDING LOANS, which is money the bank makes available to build with. This may be an outright payment of the amount considered necessary to complete the house, or it may be made in installments at different stages of construction—for example, one third for the foundation, one third for the rough framing and sewage system, etc.

Yet another way is to build part of the house with a loan or cash and then apply for a mortgage on what is already built—and use this money to complete the house.

Whichever way you finance the building, read the small print and understand the terms of the loans and mortgages, for there are many different types, and they may not all be suitable in the long run.

As soon as you own land—from the moment the deed is filed—you are liable for property taxes. As soon as you "improve" the land—for example, build a house on it—you supposedly increase its value, and will usually be taxed more. This is all ascertained by a process called ASSESSMENT. The assessors determine how much you will pay by considering how much you paid, what the house is worth, and what the local TAX RATE is. So while it helps to know in advance what the tax rate for your area is, it won't give you much idea of how much your taxes will be unless you also know the value of your proposed house.

There are a variety of taxes which you may have to pay, depending on locality. Taxes may be levied by the TOWNSHIP, TOWN or VILLAGE, and the COUNTY—the respective offices of which will give you all the information you need.

Then there are a number of special taxes which may apply, including SCHOOL TAX, WATER TAX, and SEWAGE TAX. These are likely to be administered by separate bodies, and the districts they control may or may not overlap. Once again, your local town offices will tell you what you are liable for—but find out in advance—if you don't pay, liens may be put on your house, mortgage applications denied, and your house may be auctioned off to pay the back taxes.

With the outside complete, the wiring, plumbing, insulation, and heating installed, the walls and ceilings finished, the floors laid, and the trim work complete, the house is virtually finished. While theoretically possible, it is rarely that anyone who builds his own house is ever able to say "finished!", for improvements and additions are constant. Consequently, what has been explained in this book is merely the basic structure of a house.

Subjects such as chimney building, staircase making and cabinetry, etc., would require volumes to themselves. Nevertheless, the subjects covered have been made as clear and as complete as possible.

But new developments and techniques occur continuously, and I would welcome any suggestions which might improve the usefulness of this book.